THE CROWN AND THE FIRE

The Crown and the Fire

*Meditations on the Cross
and the Life of the Spirit*

TOM WRIGHT

WILLIAM B. EERDMANS PUBLISHING COMPANY
GRAND RAPIDS, MICHIGAN

First published 1992 in Great Britain by
SPCK
Holy Trinity Church
Marylebone Road
London NW1 4DU

This edition published 1995 through special arrangement with SPCK by
Wm. B. Eerdmans Publishing Co.
255 Jefferson Ave. S.E., Grand Rapids, Michigan 49503

Printed in the United States of America

00 99 98 97 96 95   7 6 5 4 3 2 1

Library of Congress Cataloging-in-Publication Data

Wright, N. T. (Nicholas Thomas)
The crown and the fire: meditations on the Cross
and the life of the Spirit / Tom Wright.
p.   cm.
Originally published: London: SPCK, 1992.
Includes bibliographical references.
ISBN 0-8028-4131-7 (paper: alk. paper)
1. Jesus Christ — Crucifixion — Sermons. 2. Jesus Christ —
Resurrection — Sermons. 3. Holy Spirit — Sermons. 4. Sermons, English.
5. Church of England — Sermons. 6. Anglican Communion — Sermons.
7. Spiritual life — Anglican Communion — Sermons.
I. Title.
BT453.W75   1995
232.96′3 — dc20   95-30796
CIP

Unless otherwise noted, the Scripture quotations in this publication are from
the Revised Standard Version of the Bible, copyrighted 1946, 1952 © 1971,
1973 by the Division of Christian Education of the National Council of
Churches of Christ in the U.S.A., and used by permission.

The author and publisher are grateful to Faber and Faber Ltd for permission
to reproduce extracts from 'The Rock' and 'Little Gidding' by T S Eliot from
The Collected Poems of T S Eliot 1909-1962.

For Michael Lloyd

Contents

Preface

During the last decade I have tried many times to think my way through the meaning of the death and resurrection of Jesus, and the gift to his people of the Spirit. Sometimes this has been done in an academic setting, as I have wrestled with the exegesis of biblical texts or the historical task of reconstructing what actually happened during the last days of Jesus' earthly life and the first days of the church's new-found existence. Sometimes it has been done through preaching. I have not been able to keep these two tasks isolated; however, I do not think that either would have profited from my doing so. One reason for this is that throughout this last decade I have been puzzling, often with some pain and difficulty, about what it means, for me and for others, to be Christian in the modern world. I have refused to accept the easy answers offered on all sides, since time and again they have seemed to me both subbiblical and unhelpful. Instead, I have come back to the central events of the church's faith, and to some of the central passages of the Bible, and have tried to think them through at every level for myself. I am under no illusion that I have now 'arrived' at a settled or final understanding, but so many people have urged me to make these reflections more widely available that I am happy to do so now, if only as markers on my own journey and, if it may be, signposts for others.

The first half of the book consists of addresses given, in

various shapes and forms, as Good Friday meditations. Good Friday preachers have often spoken on the Seven Last Words from the Cross; I decided to focus instead on seven phrases or sentences that were addressed, so to speak, *to* the cross — words spoken to, or about, Jesus. One of the things the evangelists manage to do in telling the story of Jesus' death is to show some of the connections between the cross and what had gone before during Jesus' life, and I have tried to draw out some of those connections in my exposition. These addresses were first given, in a shorter form, at Hudson, Quebec, in 1983, in the church where my family and I were regular worshippers for four years, and to which we still look back with gratitude. They were developed at the Church of the Advent, Montreal, in 1984, and at Christ Church Cathedral, Montreal, in 1986. I reworked them for All Saints, Headington, Oxford, in 1987, and finally for St Aldate's, Oxford, in 1991. I am very grateful to the clergy of all these churches for their invitations, and to them and their parishes for their support and kind encouragement.

The second half of the book is more eclectic in background, though setting out (to my mind at least) a fairly tight line of thought. It begins with a sermon preached in St George's Cathedral, Jerusalem (and again at Tabgha, by the Sea of Galilee, where the incident which it expounds supposedly took place) in Eastertide 1989. It continues with a sermon preached first in Worcester College, Oxford, and then in Christ's College, Cambridge, in December 1990 and March 1991 respectively. The next chapter consists of a biblical exposition given to the Church of England General Synod in January 1991. This, quite unintentionally, caused something of a stir, and I hope that printing it in full here, in a wider setting which shows where it belongs in my thinking as a whole, will make my meaning clear. The book then concludes with three sermons preached in Worcester College at various times during the last five years. Once again I am grateful to those who heard the addresses and encouraged me to put them into more permanent form.

I have allowed some traces of the original settings to remain, hoping that they will add to, rather than detract from, the continued impact of what was said. I have included the biblical readings that were the basis of my reflections; if not noted otherwise, they are given in my own translation. Perhaps I should also say that I am well aware of the many problems associated with making historical claims about what happened in the life and ministry of Jesus, and am in the process of addressing those issues in other works in a different genre. I have not thought it appropriate to annotate this book with explanatory footnotes on this topic.

My thanks are due, for help with the preparation and printing of this book, to my assistant Kathleen Miles, and to the friends around the world who, in supporting the fund which has enabled me to have such assistance, have made projects like the present one possible. I would also like to record my thanks to Bishop Richard Holloway, of Edinburgh, who read a draft of the material and made helpful and encouraging comments; to my dear wife and family for their cheerful acceptance of my seemingly endless busyness; and to the editors at SPCK for their part in encouraging and enabling me to put the material into its present form. And since, indeed, encouragement is what preachers and theologians so often need and so frequently lack, I am particularly glad to dedicate this book to the Chaplain of Christ's College, Cambridge, my dear friend Michael Lloyd, from whom I have received so much of that precious commodity over the period of its growth.

Worcester College, Oxford   TOM WRIGHT
Feast of St Peter, 1991

PART ONE

THE CROWN OF THORNS

1

'If you are the Son of God . . .'

Those who passed by derided him, wagging their heads
and saying, 'You who would destroy the temple and build
it in three days, save yourself! If you are the Son of God,
come down from the cross.' So also the chief priests, with
the scribes and elders, mocked him, saying, 'He saved
others; he cannot save himself. He is the King of Israel;
let him come down now from the cross, and we will
believe in him. He trusts in God; let God deliver him now,
if he desires him; for he said, "I am the Son of God."' And
the robbers who were crucified with him also reviled him.
(Mark 15.29-32; Matthew 27.39-44 RSV)

With these words, the last and fiercest strife breaks upon the
bleeding figure on the central cross. He has been fighting
this battle one way or another all his life and now it rages around
him in full strength.

Listen to the echoes that are stirred up by this challenge: 'If
you are the Son of God, come down from the cross!' The voices
are the voices of the bystanders; but the words are the words of
Satan, the accuser, the tempter. At the start of his ministry Jesus
had heard similar words. He came up from the Jordan, with words

3

of affirmation ringing in his ears: 'You are my beloved Son, in you I am well pleased.' And at once the Spirit drove him into the wilderness, where he heard a rather different voice: 'If you are the Son of God, command these stones to be made bread'; 'If you are the Son of God, cast yourself down, and the angels will look after you.' 'If' — 'If' — perhaps you don't really believe it — perhaps you'd better do something to prove it. If you really are God's son, how could he possibly want you to go hungry all the time? If you really are God's son, surely you want everybody to see your supernatural power and believe in you (that is, of course, if you really have any power . . .). If you are the Son of God, why isn't everybody recognising you? If you really are God's son, then *what are you doing on that cross?*

The voice of Satan is often hard to recognise precisely because it appears so frequently as the voice of common sense, of prudence, of reason. Though the mediaeval paintings which display Jesus being tempted portray him engaging in argument with a visible figure, usually with hoofs and horns and a tail, anyone who has experienced fierce temptation will know that the voices we hear seem to come from the very deepest depths of our own being. So I believe it was for Jesus on that occasion. And what form does the temptation take? It comes as an attack on the very nature of the vocation and ministry of which Jesus from his early years had been conscious, and for which he had just been marked out by John in his baptism. It is the mission to be Israel's Messiah, Israel's anointed King, the one of whom it was said by God to David, 'I will be to him a Father, and he will be to me a Son', and again, 'I will designate him my firstborn, the highest of the kings on the earth.' 'You are my beloved Son: I am pleased, well pleased with you.'

But — *if* you are the Son of God — then what? What will it mean in practice? What might it involve? What *sort* of Messiahship was Jesus called to? In Jesus' baptism the issue was made quite clear. To see it we have to take a little step back.

The Jews of Jesus' day were on tiptoe with expectation. They were longing for God to step into history and lead them in triumph against their Roman overlords and oppressors. They wanted Israel to be vindicated, to be liberated, to taste again the freedom she had had when God brought her out of Egypt under the leadership of Moses, the event celebrated to this day in the festival of Passover. They wanted to smell again the scent of the victory that God had given them over the tyrant Antiochus Epiphanes two hundred years before the time of Jesus, the event celebrated to this day in the feast of Hanukkah. And sometimes, as they longed for this to happen, they focused this belief and hope in the longing that God would send them a Messiah who would be like David — who would fight against the new Goliath as their representative — who would be a warrior king, a man after David's own heart. And all this weight of longing came about not simply because of nationalist pride, nor because of racial arrogance. It came about because of the deep-rooted belief of Israel, that there was one God, and he had made the whole world, and had entered into covenant specifically with Israel. National vindication, they firmly believed, was guaranteed by the promises of God in (what we call) the Old Testament — promises which rested finally on the very character and power of God himself.

It is against *that* background that we must understand the mocking voice of Satan, via the bystanders, to the figure on the cross. *If* you are the Messiah — if you are the Son of God — then you're not *supposed* to be on a Roman cross! You're supposed to be leading your people to victory *over* the Romans! And, underneath that, the charge — Maybe you aren't really the Messiah after all. Maybe you're not the Son of God — how can you be? Whoever heard of a *crucified* Messiah? It's failed Messiahs who end up on crosses: crucifixion is what Roman soldiers usually do to poor deluded fanatics who think they're God's chosen hero and then find out, too late, that they're not after all.

And, even though the voices are those of the bystanders, we should not imagine that they failed to find an echo in Jesus' own heart and mind as he hung there, at the end of his physical and emotional strength. It is part of his full and total humanity that he should be tempted, as we all are, to doubt: to doubt himself, to doubt his vocation, to doubt God. 'Father, if it be possible, let this cup pass from me' — maybe there's another way after all: haven't I done enough? Can I be sure this is the way that you want me to go? My God, *why have you abandoned me?* Perhaps I *have* been mistaken — perhaps they're right and I've been wrong all along; perhaps I've failed them; perhaps I've failed God. We must not suppose that the mental and emotional torture of the cross was any less severe than the physical torture. And the physical torture was, as we know from contemporary Roman sources, one of the nastiest and most brutal that warped human ingenuity has ever devised.

It is with this question that we must begin, if we are to understand what the cross meant both for Jesus and for the writers of the Gospels, and what it means for us. Was Jesus on the cross a failed Messiah, or a successful Messiah? Was the cross an unfortunate and messy interval between his successful life and his triumphant resurrection, or was it the event to which his whole life pointed? Was it merely an example of innocent suffering bravely borne? Was it an historical accident which the Church then invested with a deeper significance which had no organic connection with the historical circumstances and 'meaning' — from that point of view — of the actual event? Or has the suffering and death of Jesus a meaning which possesses an organic unity with the historical events and with the meaning of Messiahship itself?

For the crowds there was no doubt. A Messiah on a cross is a failed Messiah. For Jesus, I think, there *was* doubt: perhaps the crowds were right after all, perhaps it wasn't the voice of Satan, perhaps he should have listened to Peter when he tried to reason with him, to distract him from this course. But for the writers of the Gospels there is no doubt. It is through the death of Jesus — *through* his apparent failure, through even his sense of abandonment, that God has worked out his strange purposes which ran deeper than the crowds, or the disciples, or even Jesus himself, could ever have envisaged at the time.

How this can be so we will continue to explore presently.

6

Clearly, this way of looking at things flies completely in the face of modern society, for whom 'Good Friday' has become simply 'Easter Friday', the first day of a holiday weekend. But for now, let's pause and reflect on Jesus' last great temptation — to abandon at the last minute the vocation to which he had been obedient all his life, to give way to despair and to abandon the faith by which he had lived. He could have summoned his twelve legions of angels, as he said in the garden. Or, as Job was tempted by his wife to do, he could have cursed God for betraying him. He does neither. He just hangs there, his agony squeezed out to the last drop.

For consider. C. S. Lewis, in *The Screwtape Letters*, wrote something powerfully true, of Jesus and of ourselves, when he put these words into the mouth of Screwtape, the senior devil who is giving advice to his young nephew:

> Do not be deceived, Wormwood. Our cause [that is, the Devil's cause] is never more in danger than when a human, no longer desiring, but still intending, to do our Enemy's will [that is, God's will], looks round upon a universe from which every trace of Him seems to have vanished, and asks why he has been forsaken, and still obeys.

'No longer desiring, but still intending' to do God's will. There is the key. He was tested in all points — all points — just as we are, yet without sin. There is hope within his hopelessness; there is obedience behind his doubt.

Lord Jesus Christ, Son of the Living God, on the cross You suffered not only torture and death but also sorrow and doubt; give us, we pray, such gratitude for your obedient love that, in our moments of doubt, sorrow, pain and death we may know your presence and your victory: to the glory of your great and holy name. Amen.

2

'Son, we have sought you sorrowing.'

Now his parents went to Jerusalem every year at the feast of the Passover. And when he was twelve years old, they went up according to custom; and when the feast was ended, as they were returning, the boy Jesus stayed behind in Jerusalem. His parents did not know it, but supposing him to be in the company they went a day's journey, and they sought him among their kinsfolk and acquaintances; and when they did not find him, they returned to Jerusalem, seeking him. After three days they found him in the temple, sitting among the teachers, listening to them and asking them questions; and all who heard him were amazed at his understanding and his answers. And when they saw him they were astonished; and his mother said to him, 'Son, why have you treated us so? Behold, your father and I have been looking for you anxiously.' And he said to them, 'How is it that you sought me? Did you not know that I must be in my Father's house?' And they did not understand the saying which he spoke to them. And he went down with them and came to Nazareth, and was obedient to them; and his mother kept all these things in her heart. And Jesus increased in wisdom and in stature, and in favour with God and man. (Luke 2.41-52 RSV)

It was not only Jesus, we may suppose, who went through the agony of doubt and despair on Good Friday. The disciples had hoped that he would be the one to redeem Israel. That was why they had been following him through the dusty roads of Galilee and Judaea these many months. They had never really understood what he had been trying to tell them about what would happen when they got to Jerusalem — how could they? Their world-view simply couldn't contain it. Perhaps he was using some strange mythological language: speaking in riddles, or metaphors, that their untutored minds couldn't grasp. All this stuff about the Son of Man being under an obligation to die at the hands of the Romans . . . How could a Roman cross be the intended climax of the work of redemption that they knew — they believed — they hoped — he had come to complete? He must mean something else, and they couldn't figure it out. Well, now it was happening, and they still hadn't figured it out: they were away in hiding somewhere, with their dreams and hopes in shreds. But *we* may begin to find our way to the answer that they couldn't see if we focus attention on one follower who *was* there, right to the end: Jesus' own mother.

For Mary, just as for Jesus, the crucifixion represents the culmination of a theme which had been growing within her experience for some while, the complete statement of a tragic melody heard up until now only in fragments. Consider the path by which *she* had come. As a faithful Jewish girl, there can be no doubt that Gabriel's announcement would indicate to her the birth, from her womb, of the Messiah who would liberate his oppressed people. How much she understood of Simeon's warning, that a sword would pierce her soul, we cannot say. We then meet her, in the above passage, in the three days' agony of having lost her twelve-year-old treasure. No parent will miss the sickening panic in that simple narrative. A day's walk away from Jerusalem, and all is well. Then suddenly — where is he? Isn't he with you? Oh, he must be around somewhere — push the horrible fear away if possible, don't panic, keep hoping. Haven't you seen him? Hasn't anybody seen him? Where — where is he? The frantic rush back to Jerusalem, all thought of festival and holiday suddenly vanished. Then three days — think of it, three *days* — of looking everywhere, in a city still packed with pilgrims, tourists, con-men, pickpockets, soldiers, whores, merchants, priests, drunkards — and somewhere, like a needle in a haystack, an innocent twelve-year-old from a country town. He's only twelve! How can he be all right? Where has he been staying? Supposing . . .

And the last place they think of looking is the place where it matters. There he sits, surrounded by the greybeards, listening to them and asking them questions. He is old enough to be precocious, even while being young enough to be precious to his mother. 'Son,' she says, 'we have sought you sorrowing.' And all the reply she gets is that he had to be about his Father's business — an implied rebuke, in Luke's telling of the story, to her mention of Joseph as his father. He has to be there, didn't you know? — debating with the learned in the temple, growing up in wisdom and stature, and in favour both with God and with man. 'How is it that you did not know?'

The puzzle only deepens as he grows up further, meeting her with rude shocks: 'Woman, what have you to do with me? My hour has not yet come.' 'Who are my mother and my brothers? Anyone who does the will of God is my mother, my sister, my brother.' Mary looks on in that strange and beautiful scene at the wedding in Cana of Galilee, while Jesus answers the need she expresses but rebukes her for expressing it. She comes with her other sons to find Jesus in the crowd down at the tavern, asking for him, wanting to find him — 'Son, we have sought you sorrowing'; and all the answer she gets is that as far as he's concerned family ties are not important in the Kingdom of God. What kind of son is that? What kind of Messiah is that? Mary has to watch in horror as her well-brought-up son takes up with the most disreputable of the rabble in the town. He makes friends with

11

people on the wrong side, with people of the wrong sort; he gets on easy terms with the quislings, the tax-men who were collaborating with the occupying forces. He seems to exercise a strange fascination and attraction for young women of quite the wrong sort. And as we meet her at the foot of the cross we have therefore a sense of history repeating itself. For three years now, not just three days, she has sought him sorrowing: and now she finds him at last. So this is where it has all led:

> Woman, what have you to do with me?
> My hour has come, now, but not the way you wanted:
> All I can do this time is change the water into
> Blood: your blood, from my veins,
> From the wound in
> Your soul and my side.

He has run away again: she thought she knew him, and now she finds she didn't. *He* is the prodigal son, off in the far country, wasting his spiritual treasure with harlots, feeding his pearls to the swine, to the unclean rabble, to murderers and thieves like these two: 'Son, we have sought you sorrowing.' And, despite the modesty of paintings and crucifixes, it is a fact that men were crucified naked: a matter of shame to the Jew for whom nakedness was an indecent pagan affectation when playing sport, and double shame to the Jewish mother for whom the circumcision of her firstborn son *had* been the proudest day of her life.

Think of the Magnificat:

> My soul magnifies the Lord,
> and my spirit exults in God my saviour.

Now think of it in a minor key:

> My soul is in pain before the Lord,
> my spirit is in anguish in God my deceiver.

The taunts directed at Jesus cut into her, too: If you are the Mother of God, bid him now come down from the cross, and all generations will call you blessed. Gabriel had never warned her about this — never let her in on the secret that to carry God in your womb was to court disaster. With all that love, who would have thought there could be such pain? What is the relationship between love and pain, anyway? In Mary is focused sharply the pride and the hope of Israel, and now the disappointment and horror of Israel. Here was the one to redeem God's people! Blessed is the King who comes in the name of the Lord! The agony Jesus experiences on Palm Sunday, weeping over Jerusalem even while the crowds are singing Hosanna, is acted out by Mary on Good Friday, weeping over her son as the crowds are yelling for his blood. What is he doing? Hadn't she known all along that he was sailing close to the wind, keeping such disreputable company, offending the scribes and Pharisees, challenging the sacred law of God in respect of the kosher regulations and the sabbath principles? What did he think he was doing? He was supposed to be upholding and vindicating Israel, not tearing her institutions apart! Maybe she had been wrong, too; maybe she had just imagined Gabriel's visit; maybe it was just her wishful thinking: after all, whoever heard of God — even Israel's God — actually being born as a baby . . . and didn't every Jewish girl dream of becoming the mother of the Messiah? Maybe she'd just let her dreams run away with her . . .

If Jesus presents an enigmatic figure in the Gospels, so does Mary. A woman full of grace, to be called blessed indeed by all generations, to be called — as her cousin Elizabeth said — 'the mother of my Lord', and then by the later Church *Theotokos,* the God-Bearer, Mother of God. But Mary is also a thoroughly human being, sharing the misconceptions and puzzles and consequent pain of the Jewish people of her day, whom, as the Messiah's mother, she represents. She has given birth to the redeemer of the world; but, *how* is he to redeem the world? And what will she feel when that comes about? There is the sword in her heart also.

Come back once more to the scene at that Passover when Jesus was twelve years old. In my mind's eye I can see Luke's painting of the scene as though on a canvas. Jesus sits just off-centre to the left, the greybeard doctors and scribes sitting around him so that the eye is drawn to him at one side, an enigma in himself. But the young man Jesus is looking away from them, to the other side of the picture. And in the foreground to the right there rush in Mary and Joseph, their faces a mixture of three-day sleepless tiredness, worry, relief, anger, love, bewilderment, themselves an enigma as they burst in on the scene of tranquil scholarship. And as the two enigmas, Jesus and Mary, fix their eyes on one another, a third enigma is created, which Luke puts into words: *How is it that you did not know?* It is the sort of picture which demands that you sit and look at it for a long time. You will not easily exhaust its strange power, even when the tension relaxes and Jesus goes home like a good boy, and grows up in wisdom and stature and in favour with God and man.

Because if Mary represents Israel, she also represents the world: the world which yearns and groans for redemption, and then cannot understand Redemption when he comes to her, clothed in her own flesh and blood, refusing to accept her categories, her oversimplifications, refusing to be cowed by her panic, her wrong expectations, even her anger. He came into the world; and the world was made through him, but the world knew him not. He came to his own, and his own received him not. This is how it always was, and how it always will be until the day when every knee shall bow at his name. He is that for which Israel longed, for which the world longs, and yet his coming seems to bring, not joy, but only pain. The Jews knew this to the extent that one of their great pictures for the arrival of the last days, the days of redemption, was the powerful and shocking image of a woman in the act of giving birth. It is an image which speaks of great hope, the promise of new life; but which speaks just as powerfully (especially to the ancient world innocent of our modern surgery and drugs) of risk and fear, of sharp and terrible pain, of forces suddenly unleashed which, though life-giving in intent,

14

seem to carry death at their heart. Mary, called to be the Mother
of God, is called to take upon herself the labour pains of the new
age, not at Bethlehem only, but in Jerusalem at Passover-time, and
that not once but twice, at the climactic points of her whole life.
'Son — we have sought you sorrowing.'

We are not told that she said anything as she stood at the
foot of the cross. Jesus, we are told, gives her the beloved disciple
to care for her in his place. She is about to have another three
days of agony, mourning the loss of Israel's hope and consolation,
another three days before love's bright pain will fill her life, as
once before it filled her body, not of the will of man, but of God.
But the essence of the scene is encapsulated in the look that passes
once more between the enigmatic Son and the enigmatic Mother:
'Son, we have sought you sorrowing' meeting 'How is it that you
did not know?' And the meaning of it all is not found by ignoring
or bypassing the bitterness and puzzle and doubt but by looking
deep within them. This is the answer Mary receives, after all these
years:

> Here he is; here is your disappointment, your runaway Son:
> Did you not know that he must be about
>   his Father's business,
> Arguing with love and pain and reconciling them,
> Lifted up high in wisdom and stature
> And in anguish both of God and Man?

And we too are called to be *Theotokoi,* God-bearers. We are,
in ways that we will explore later, called to be those through
whom God's redeeming love will still come to birth in the world.
For that reason, and because of the model we have in Mary, we
are not to be amazed if at the same time a sword should pierce
our hearts also. That is by no means a sign that we are on the
wrong road. On the contrary. It is when we share the groaning
of all creation that, according to St Paul, we hear the Spirit
groaning yet deeper within us, assuring us that we are the children
of God, heirs of God, fellow-heirs with the risen Christ. Better to

be puzzled, like Mary, at the strange things that Jesus is doing to me and in me than settle for an easily grasped half-truth with neither depth nor power. We are called to be the bearers of God-in-Christ to his world, pondering in our hearts the mysteries we do not yet understand, seeking him in and through our own sorrow, ready to search for our young Lord wherever he may be found, whether discussing with the learned, partying with the riffraff, or dying with the outcasts. How is it that *we* did not know?

Almighty God, by the agony of Mary teach us to see your hand at work not only in our joy, but in our pain; not only in our victories, but in our defeats; not only in our strength, but in our weakness; not only in our hopes, but in our disappointments; not only in our lives, but in our deaths; that we may believe in your love revealed on Calvary, and, believing, may know your peace which passes understanding: through Jesus Christ, your crucified Son, our Lord. Amen.

3

'This man has done
nothing wrong.'

One of the criminals who were hanged blasphemed and
said, 'Aren't you the Messiah? Save yourself, and us!' But
the other rebuked him: 'Don't you fear God, since you are
under the same condemnation? And in our case it's fair
enough: we are getting what we deserve: but this man has
done nothing wrong.' And he said, 'Jesus, remember me
when you come in your Kingdom.' And he said to him,
'Truly, I say to you, today you will be with me in Paradise.'
(Luke 23.39-43)

This man has done nothing wrong. With this story, told by
Luke with typical brevity and yet with an equally typical
evocative quality, we begin to put the picture together — to see
how it is that, on the cross, Jesus was not a failed Messiah, but
was, paradoxically, the true Messiah: to see why not only the
cross, but the whole pattern of events leading up to it, was indeed
the saving plan and purpose of the creator God. And we must
begin where we ended last time, with Mary's dilemma. The purpose of putting Jesus on a cross was to say — Here he is, this

Messiah: this is what happens to failed Messiahs! And the purpose of crucifying him between the two thieves was to say — That's the sort of man he is! In fact, calling them 'thieves' as we normally do obscures the matter. The word in Greek is *lestes* — a word which the Jewish historian Josephus uses of revolutionary Jews who used force in the attempt to rid Palestine of Roman rule. There were many of them in Jesus' day; a kind of holy brigand, so keen to see Israel's God triumph in the world that they were ready to help his cause on its way with violence, murder, and what we would call acts of terrorism. The Romans didn't crucify burglars or handbag snatchers. They did crucify revolutionaries. And so putting Jesus on the cross says — This is who he is, just another rabble-rouser, deceiving the people, pretending that he's the one who God is going to use to lead us to freedom. He's a rebel against Rome; he's a false king; he's a would-be rival to Caesar. And so, ironically, the Romans wanted to get rid of him because he was a nationalist Messiah, and the Jews wanted to get rid of him because he wasn't.

Do you see how this fits in with Mary's problem? 'He was numbered with the transgressors', said Jesus of himself the night he was betrayed, quoting Isaiah's prophecy about Israel, the servant who would bear the sins of the many (Isaiah 53). Numbered with transgressors — yes, and that's what's been going on all along! Look and see where Jesus is, and you'll find him in the middle of a motley, disreputable, dishonest, disrespectable crew. But what happens? The dying thief puts his finger on the point: 'This man has done nothing wrong.' He is among us; he looks, outwardly, as though he is cursed as we are cursed, unclean as we are unclean. But something strange is going on. Jesus on the cross *is* — Jesus the coming King. And Jesus on the cross is Jesus the *saving* King: 'Lord, remember me when you come into your Kingdom.' 'Today,' replies Jesus, 'you will be with me in Paradise.' And that 'today', in its setting, sends us back again to the earlier parts of Luke's Gospel, in which we can see, acted out as it were in advance, the drama of the cross and its inner meaning.

Think of the story of Zacchaeus. Jesus comes to Jericho, and little Zacchaeus, who just wanted to watch the fun from a safe distance, suddenly discovers that he's playing host to an unexpected guest. Now nice people didn't invite themselves to lunch with Zacchaeus. Real Messiahs don't eat with tax collectors. Zacchaeus was a swindler and a cheat, a master of sharp and shady financial dealings. He was in the pay of the occupying Roman forces, a quisling and a hated traitor. He was known as a 'sinner', and anyone — and this is the point — anyone who eats with a 'sinner' becomes tainted with that sin, becomes a 'sinner' himself. That's why the people outside Zacchaeus' house look on and say, in horror and amazement — He has gone in to eat with a man who is a sinner! This man who talks about the Kingdom of God, and seems to be actually bringing it with him wherever he goes, has gone to eat with Zacchaeus of all people. But then the miracle happens — the miracle-in-advance which foreshadows the miracle of Calvary itself. Jesus and Zacchaeus come out of the house and face the crowds, and Jesus declares: 'Today salvation has come to this house; he too is a Son of Abraham.' The Son of Man came to seek and to save the lost. That's why he's here. Jesus is numbered, voluntarily, with the transgressors: but instead of that making him a sinner too, it means that sinners are rescued. He somehow takes from them the stain of their sin, the pollution they are carrying, and his purity and innocence go out in strength to heal, to forgive, to rescue.

You can see exactly the same point in the healing miracles. Here is Jesus touching a leper: now you just don't do that, or if you do you become ritually unclean yourself, and quite possibly contract the disease into the bargain. But somehow Jesus' cleanness and wholeness infect the leper, instead of his being infected by the leper. So too with the woman who had the issue of blood. She had been ritually unclean through that disease for twelve years. Every bed she lay on would be unclean: every dish out of which she ate would have to be either broken, or scoured within an inch of its life. And anybody who touched her, or whom she touched, would automatically become unclean too, and would have to go through the tedious business of ritual purification.

And yet she comes and touches — Jesus. Of course she is embarrassed when Jesus turns round and says, 'Who touched me?' But again the miracle happens. 'Some one touched me,' he says, 'I can tell, because power has gone out of me.' That's the point: the special power of Jesus, the power not of force but of love, not of oppression but of health and purity, is stronger than the ritual uncleanness she had had for so many years.

The same thing is true when Jesus raises to life the son of the widow at Nain. He walks forward and touches the bier on which the dead man lay. Again, you don't do that unless you want to become ritually unclean, impure. But Jesus doesn't contract uncleanness. It just doesn't stick to him. Instead, power once more flows out in the opposite direction. He, as it were, takes human uncleannesses, so that other humans can take his wholeness. He absorbs our impurity in himself so that it becomes lost without trace, and his own purity flows into us instead.

And this is one of the main clues which Luke gives us in his Gospel to help us understand the meaning of the cross. In this is hidden the first answer to the puzzle and despair of Mary. She had seen her precious son apparently becoming a sinner, keeping company with Mary Magdalene and Zacchaeus and all the rest. What she had not seen, apparently, was the inner healing and new life which he had given to the former prostitute and the crooked tax-gatherer. Now, at Calvary, she sees her son, God's chosen one, dying the death of the criminal, the revolutionary. He is dying the death of the failed rebel against Rome. She does *not* see, yet, what Luke allows us to see — the rebel turning to Jesus on the cross and finding in him a new life even in the midst of death. She sees Jesus as a failed man, a failed Messiah: Luke invites us to see that *in that very failure,* as it seemed, Jesus is in fact succeeding in the *real* task he has been set.

We can see this most clearly in the trial before Pilate. The Jewish leaders arraign Jesus on three charges. He is leading the people astray, they say; he is forbidding people to pay taxes to Caesar, and he is giving himself out as Messiah, as King. There is heavy irony in this presentation by Luke. Luke's readers know very well that these are the very things which Jesus has *not* been doing. He has been healing, restoring, giving new life; he has explicitly refused to forbid paying taxes; and he has always left the fact of his redefined Messiahship to be inferred, to be worked out, by those who had eyes to see. He has never gone around announcing it to all and sundry. He couldn't do that. It would have been totally misunderstood. People would have inevitably heard it in a thoroughly nationalist sense — as though he was coming to spearhead that movement of violent resistance against Rome for which so many Jews longed. But Jesus has not come to underwrite Israel's nationalist ambitions, to support her policy of an exclusivist purity which kept out of the chosen people all those who through birth, or through sin, or through physical ailments, were less than fully qualified for membership in God's people. He has come to seek and to save the lost, and right there on the cross *he is doing it.* 'This man has done nothing wrong.' This, paradoxically, is where he is meant to be, is where God wants him to be. He has come on his Father's business, to bring God's own love right down to the level of those who most desperately need it. He is numbered with the transgressors, so that transgressors may be with him in Paradise. He has become what we are, so that we might become what he is. For our sake he became poor, so that we by his poverty might become rich.

Jesus, the innocent one, the one person who has done nothing wrong, the one innocent of the crimes of which Israel as a whole was guilty, has become identified with rebel Israel who represents God's whole rebel world; with us who are rebels, unclean, unfaithful, unloving, unholy — so that he may take that sin as it were into himself and deal with it, and give us instead his holiness as a robe, his purity as a gift and a power. This is the real meaning of Messiahship. He has come to represent Israel, all right: but Israel's problem is deeper than her national plight, and one who comes from God to represent her cannot do so in a merely military fashion, like David taking on Goliath on behalf of the people of God. The one who comes from God to represent Israel can only do so by taking Israel's shame and blame on to

21

himself. And, as Israel was called by God to represent the world, a vocation which had been almost totally lost sight of in the headlong rush towards rebellion against Rome, towards self-defence and self-preservation at all costs, so now Israel's representative cannot possibly be the one to lead the fight against the national enemy. He has come to do for Israel, and for the world, what neither Israel nor the world could do for itself. He has come to die the death of the world, so that the world through him might be saved.

Who is the real enemy, then? The real enemy is not Rome, the political enemy of the people of God. The real enemy is Satan, sin, and death — the unseen spiritual enemies then and now, for whom outward political enslavement is simply a metaphor, a reminder. Satan, in his fury at being faced with a foe who has identified where the real problem lies and is marching resolutely to meet it and deal with it, is desperately trying to distract him, to turn him aside even at this final moment. Mary, through her anguish, sees her son dragged down to the level of the thief and the rebel. And now the rebel, of all people, sees the innocent King coming in his Kingdom, ruling victoriously from the cross over sin and death. And it is the meaning of that Kingdom that we will soon be exploring further. For now, let us remember Jesus' identification with those who, like ourselves, were only too aware of their sin, their failure, their lack of wholeness and cleanness: and let us hold that identification before our minds in grateful and humble prayer.

Almighty God, we thank you with all our heart that on the cross Jesus became one with us in our sin, so that we might, despite that sin, share the life of your Kingdom. Enable us, we pray, to be truly grateful, and to live not as unforgiven sinners, despairing in our own weakness, but as your forgiven sons and daughters, rejoicing in your power to save and cleanse and give life: to the glory of your great and holy name. Amen.

4

'What I have written,
I have written.'

So they took Jesus, and he went out, bearing his own cross, to the place called the place of a skull, which is called in Hebrew Golgotha. There they crucified him, and with him two others, one on either side, and Jesus between them. Pilate also wrote a title and put it on the cross; it read 'Jesus of Nazareth, the King of the Jews.' Many of the Jews read this title, for the place where Jesus was crucified was near the city; and it was written in Hebrew, in Latin, and in Greek. The chief priests of the Jews then said to Pilate, 'Do not write "The King of the Jews," but "This man said, I am King of the Jews." Pilate answered, 'What I have written, I have written.' (John 19.17-22 RSV)

Pontius Pilate was not noted for his tact. The Jewish historian Josephus records many instances of his blunt, offensive, and inept handling of the Jews, and this incident about the title on the cross illustrates the point very nicely. The title on a cross — a sort of crude placard or notice fastened above the head of the convicted person — was placed there to tell onlookers the nature of the crime which the man had committed. Thus if a slave had stolen something from his master, he might be labelled 'Runaway slave', 'Thief', and so on. In Jesus' case the 'crime' was summed up in the ironic words 'The King of the Jews', so often summarised in paintings by the four letters INRI, standing for the Latin *Iesous Nazaraius Rex Ioudaiorum,* Jesus of Nazareth the King of the Jews. And in that title, and its double meaning, is hidden a good deal of the significance of the cross.

For Pilate this was, no doubt, just another way of mocking the Jewish nation and its rulers. 'This is what I think of you: you're a bunch of no-good rebels. Any king of yours deserves to end up like this.' The king stands, as it were, for the people. Pilate is saying, 'This is how you'll all end up if you don't watch out.' Not surprisingly, the Jewish leaders protest, but Pilate has made up his mind. 'What I have written, I have written.'

Now obviously the evangelists wish to draw our attention to this statement about Jesus, and I think if we probe a bit deeper we can see why. To begin with, there is something very odd about Jesus being put to death as a political messianic pretender, though that is what the title, and the whole of the trial scene before Pilate, seems to imply. Although when Jesus is on trial before the chief priests the charge has other dimensions too — notably that of blasphemy — when he appears at the Roman governor's tribunal the accusation, as we saw, is that he has been a political rabble-rouser, forbidding people to give tribute to Caesar, saying that he is the Messiah, a king. The odd part is that, according to all our sources, that is precisely what Jesus had not done: on the contrary, that is exactly the sort of leader many Jews — including, quite probably, most of the disciples — had wanted him to be; and it was a nationalist, revolutionary attitude like that which he had resolutely refused to adopt. The oddity, the irony, is that Jesus is apparently going to his death on a charge of which he is innocent but of which most of his contemporaries are in fact guilty — a charge of anti-Roman nationalist sedition.

Here again we see that aspect of the cross which emerged from the story of the dying thief, and which of course is highlighted particularly by the Barabbas incident. Barabbas was guilty of the sort of violent rabble-rousing of which Jesus stands accused. He goes free, and the innocent Jesus dies quite literally in his place. And through it all, the evangelists are saying to us, their readers: in the death of Jesus, the innocent one is dying in place of the guilty. Surely he has borne our griefs, and carried our sorrows. He was wounded for our transgressions, and bruised for our iniquities. He dies, we go free.

A further ironic twist is supplied if we link the charge against Jesus with the Satanic temptations we were thinking about earlier. Satan was desperately trying to tempt Jesus to become the sort of Messiah the people wanted. But if he had become that sort of leader — now think about this — *he would probably have ended up on a cross just the same:* only this time the charge of 'rebel' would be true, and he would indeed have died as a failed Messiah in both senses, a failure from the people's point of view, and a disobedient failure from God's point of view. We will come back to this in the next meditation.

But to return to that title on the cross. Pilate's comment on Jesus is added now to those of the bystanders, of Mary, of the penitent rebel on the neighbouring cross. As far as Pilate is concerned, Jesus is a political Messiah, and a failed one at that. Jesus has stood up for the Kingdom of God, and the kingdom of Caesar has come down on him like a ton of bricks. Jesus has rendered to God what was God's: now, on the cross, he is rendering to Caesar what is Caesar's.

Because, you see, the gospel which Jesus preached is a direct challenge to the power structures of this world. We do not often, perhaps, think of it like that. Children of our times as we are, we like to keep politics and religion in separate, and watertight, compartments. But try selling that line to a Jew of the first century! Or try selling it to a Roman emperor, for whom the worship of the national gods was a vital part of what constituted obedient allegiance to himself! Religion was woven tightly into the whole social fabric of the world, as it has been at almost all times and almost all places in human history, with only the last two centuries in certain parts of the Western world being exceptions, and even then the split is only skin deep. Result: challenge the religion, and you challenge the society. Summon people to a new allegiance to God, and you weaken their allegiance to Caesar. Or, as it may be, summon nationalist rebels to a new allegiance to God and you weaken their allegiance to the rebel cause, as they discover that their rebellion proceeded not from faith and trust but from fear and bruised arrogance. There you have, in a nutshell, the historical and political reasons why Jesus was crucified.

So when we say that the gospel of Jesus posed a threat to the established power structures, we cannot imagine that he was simply offering an alternative political solution. He wasn't coming to propose a left-wing alternative to a right-wing government, or vice versa. He wasn't even — in fact, he most emphatically wasn't — offering a Jewish nationalist alternative to a Roman colonialist system, though that as we have seen was what his contemporaries wanted him to do, and it was what the Romans assumed he'd been trying to do, and it's what many people today have imagined he was really doing. That's why Pilate was so surprised when he examined Jesus and came to the conclusion that he wasn't that sort of Messiah. Pilate simply didn't have the categories to put Jesus into. He couldn't make head or tail of him.

So what was Jesus offering, then? He was offering a new world. Up until now, the world had been shared out among the rulers of the world. Caesar and his rivals had parcelled the world out between them. And the Jewish nation had been getting more and more frustrated, waiting for God to step in and give them their place in the sun. And behind Caesar and his rivals, and behind the Jewish nationalism too, we hear a more sinister claim, made by an old acquaintance in the wilderness: 'To you I will give all this authority and its glory; for it has been delivered to me, and I give it to whom I will.' The claim of Satan is that human beings have allowed him to rule over them instead of letting God be their god. When people worship Caesar, they are really worshipping Satan. When people make the state a god, they make it a demon. We see it all around us in our world, too, even though

26

a good many people would mock at the idea of there being actual demons. We, too, appeal to the 'forces' of economics, of political theories, of sociology; or, at a personal level, to the forces of aggression and sexuality; and increasingly people talk about such forces as if they are known to be things that it is pointless to resist. The pattern is that of paganism, even though in polite society we ignore the lunatic fringe of real pagans.

God's intended order for the world was quite different. He intended the rulers of the world — and those things we call 'forces', too — to be obedient to him, to put their energies to serve his purposes of love and creativity. Rulers who know what they are about will rule their people in humility, knowing full well that they themselves are responsible to God for what they do with their delegated authority. But when the rulers begin to forget God, they imagine that they are responsible to no one but themselves; and the result is that they begin to take the place of God. And when the state becomes a god, then look out, because it becomes at that moment, not God, but a demon. Human beings have given their proper authority to it: it has usurped their place in God's world.

So when Jesus dies as a failed, bizarre, nonpolitical political Messiah, Pilate embodies for a moment the apparent triumph of Satan over Jesus. 'This is your hour,' says Jesus to the soldiers in the garden, 'This is your hour, and the power of darkness.' Satan had offered Jesus the kingdoms of the world, on one condition: that he fall down and worship him. Jesus had refused to do so, and the cross is the direct result of that refusal. The kingdoms of the world reject him, and kill him. And not only Rome, either: there was no room for Jesus not only in the Roman empire of his day, but also in the official Judaism of the day. In the trial before Caiaphas, Jesus is faced again with Satan's question: 'Are you indeed the Christ, the Son of the Blessed?' (If so, by implication, what are you doing here before me on trial for your life?) Judaism had itself become, in its official front and in much of its popular aspiration, a world power just like Caesar. We must not imagine that when Jesus was put to death it was by second-rate religious nonsense and third-rate political ploys. It was Judaism, and Rome, that put Jesus on the cross: the highest religion, and the finest political and governmental system, that the world of that time had ever seen.

That tells us something very important about God's verdict on the whole world of human affairs. But, beyond that, we can see that the whole life and ministry of Jesus has indeed been a battle with demons. Not just with the evil spirits who possessed poor lunatic souls whom Jesus set free, though they were real enough in their own way. No: the battle has been with the rulers of the world, the power structures who have organised themselves and their authority so that there is no room for God in the world, so that they have sewn up all the gaps and left him out of the equation, leaving themselves unopposed masters of the field. Jesus, then, has come not to offer yet one more political alternative but to break the stranglehold that the powers have on the world. He offers a new world, a world in which God is God and human beings are set free to be human beings.

And what happens to him in consequence? The rulers of this world, acting out Satan's revenge upon this one who dares to raid the strong man's house and plunder his goods, take away his power and dignity and life: they strip him naked, and hold him up to contempt in public, dancing round him and celebrating their triumph over him: 'You who would destroy the temple and rebuild it in three days, save yourself!' 'What I have written, I have written.' But it is at precisely this point that Satan has overreached himself: because the cross is, in point of fact, not the world's victory over Jesus, but Jesus' victory over the world. Here is the mystery, the secret, one might almost say the *cunning*, of the deep love of God: that it is bound to draw on to itself the hatred and pain and shame and anger and bitterness and rejection of the world, but to draw all those things on to itself is precisely the means, chosen from all eternity by the generous, loving God, by which to rid his world of the evils which have resulted from human abuse of God-given freedom.

Listen to what St Paul says, taking the brutal facts of the

cross and turning them inside out: 'God cancelled the bond which stood against us, with its legal demands: he set it aside, nailing it to the cross.' That is to say: The world, and the rulers of the world, had you in their grip. Satan had you in his power, and you could not escape. But Jesus took that bondage upon himself: it is all there in the charge which was nailed over the cross, and in Pilate's cynical use of his authority: 'What I have written, I have written.' Jesus took it on himself; and, being the one person who had never in fact submitted to the rulers of the world, the one who all along had been free of them, who had lived as a free human being, obedient to God and lovingly sovereign over the world, he beat them at their own game. He drew on to himself the despotic fury which was crushing the world, and, by dying to it without submitting to it, he defeated it. He remained obedient to the end, because his love went right to the end. That is why St Paul concludes triumphantly: *He* stripped the *rulers! He* made a public example of *them;* God, in Christ, celebrated *his* triumph over the prince of the world.

The cross is not a defeat, but a victory. It is the dramatic reassertion of the fact that God's love is sovereign, that the rulers of the world do not have the last word, that the Kingdom of God has defeated the kingdom of Satan, that the kingdoms of the world have now become, in principle, the Kingdom of our God, and of his Messiah: and he shall reign for ever and ever. The nations rage and fume, and plot against God and against his anointed. But the one who dwells in heaven laughs them to scorn, and replies: 'Yet I have set my King upon my holy hill.' But the holy hill in question is not now Zion, the temple mount, the joy of the whole earth. It is the ugly little hill about a mile further west, just outside the wall of the old city. That is where the King of the Jews is enthroned, his brow still smarting with the crown of thorns, his cross the sign of God's victory over the world.

Lord Christ, almighty Saviour, we cry to you for help against our strong enemy. You are the Stronger than the strong; deliver us, we pray, from the evil one, and take sole possession of our hearts and minds: that filled with your Spirit we may henceforth devote our lives to your service, and find there our perfect freedom. Break today the power of all tyrants who usurp your rightful authority and who oppress men and women, and set up instead your Kingdom of love and peace: for the honour of your great name. Amen.

5

'The King of the Jews'

Behold, my servant shall prosper, he shall be exalted and lifted up, and shall be very high. As many were astonished at him — his appearance was so marred, beyond human semblance, and his form beyond that of the sons of men — so shall he startle many nations; kings shall shut their mouths because of him; for that which has not been told them they shall see, and that which they have not heard they shall understand.

Who has believed our report? And to whom has the arm of the Lord been revealed? For he grew up before him like a young plant, and like a root out of dry ground; he had no form or comeliness that we should look at him, and no beauty that we should desire him. He was despised and rejected by men; a man of sorrows, and acquainted with grief; and as one from whom men hide their faces he was despised, and we esteemed him not.

Surely he has borne our griefs, and carried our sorrows; yet we esteemed him stricken, smitten by God, and afflicted. But he was wounded for our transgressions, he was bruised for our iniquities; upon him was the chastisement that made us whole, and with his stripes we are healed. All we like sheep have gone astray; we have turned every one to his own way; and the Lord has laid on him the iniquity of us all.

He was oppressed, and he was afflicted, yet he opened not his mouth; like a lamb that is led to the slaughter, and like a sheep before its shearers is dumb, so he opened not his mouth. By oppression and judgment he was taken away; and as for his generation, who considered that he was cut off out of the land of the living, stricken for the transgression of my people? And they made his grave with the wicked, and with a rich man in his death, although he had done no violence, and there was no deceit in his mouth.

Yet it was the will of the Lord to bruise him; he has put him to grief; when he makes himself an offering for sin, he shall see his offspring, he shall prolong his days; the will of the Lord shall prosper in his hand. He shall see the fruit of the travail of his soul and be satisfied; by his knowledge shall the righteous one, my servant, make many to be accounted righteous; and he shall bear their iniquities. Therefore I will divide him a portion with the great, and he shall divide the spoil with the strong; because he poured out his soul to death, and was numbered with the transgressors; yet he bore the sin of many, and made intercession for the transgressors. (Isaiah 52.13–53.12 RSV)

We must now probe closer to the centre of the real drama that was taking place on Good Friday, behind the shouting and the pain, the mockery and the misunderstandings. How could it be that on the cross Jesus was being, not a failed Messiah, but a successful Messiah? How could it be that he was not there being defeated by the world but was actually celebrating his own triumph over Satan, the world, and all their powers?

If we are to understand the deepest meaning of the cross, we must take a deep breath and plunge back into the old Jewish beliefs to which Jesus was heir, the promises of the Old Testament which give shape and meaning to the strange events not only of Good Friday but of the entire Gospel story. The Gospels are written, not to be self-supporting stories in themselves, but to be the climax of a much larger story — the story of Israel, and behind that the story of the whole world.

What was God's purpose for Israel, for the Jews? A hard question, you might think. But from the Old Testament as a whole the answer begins to emerge. God called Israel to be the means of dealing with the sin of the world. If you like, God called Abraham to undo the sin of Adam. Israel was to be the true humanity, the people in whom God's purposes for the world would be fulfilled. Israel was to be the light of the world, the city which would be set on a hill and not hidden, the salt of the earth, that which brought out of God's world its true flavour, or which showed it up in its true colours. Just as humankind is created to bear God's image before the world, that is, to rule the world as God's representative, so Israel is to be God's representative to the rest of the human race.

And what was true of Israel was to be true supremely of her King, her anointed one, David and his heirs and successors. Solomon, David's son, is described as the one whose wisdom and splendour exceeds that of all the kings of the earth, so that the Queen of the South comes and pays him homage. Solomon becomes, in Jewish thought, the picture of the truly wise man, who serves God in complete obedience and so can rule wisely and justly over God's world. And though the Old Testament writers knew as well as we do that Solomon in himself was actually a more ambiguous figure than that, just as his father David had been, they maintain and preserve this picture because it holds out before Israel the truth — that humankind, and particularly Israel, and especially Israel's Davidic King, is to be God's chosen means of ruling over his world.

But how were God's purposes to be fulfilled through the nation and her King? It gradually dawned upon the inspired writers of the Old Testament that, though Israel had been called to solve the world's problem, to undo the sin of Adam, Israel as a whole was unequal to the task, was in fact incapable of even attempting it. Because Israel herself was part of the problem. It was not merely the world that needed redeeming. Israel *herself* needed to be redeemed, remade. There must be, as Jeremiah said, a *new* covenant which will deal with the real problem — the problem which was not only Adam's but also Israel's, and which manifests itself now as national arrogance, with Israel's assumption of automatic superiority over the nations of the world whom she was called to serve. In the new covenant, the problem, whose short name is sin, can at last be fully and finally dealt with, so that Jew and Gentile alike can find forgiveness and attain that truly human life which God wills for those made in his image.

But how can this now be achieved? Who can step in and do for Israel and the world what needs to be done, but what neither Israel nor the world can do for itself? To this question the prophet Isaiah answers, in the name of the Lord: *Behold, my servant*. He describes a strange figure. I don't think Isaiah himself knew who it was he was talking about; the servant is as it were a construct, on the one hand conforming to the ideal Israel, and thus given royal characteristics as Israel's King, but on the other hand standing over against Israel, standing in for her. He comes to do what the nation as a whole, and all previous Davidic kings, have failed to do. As the prophet sees in his extraordinary vision, he will die a vicarious death so that those whom he represents may not die; he it is through whom the covenant will be renewed, so that the message of good news may resound throughout the world, out beyond Israel to the islands and coastlands far away.

So the prophet sees that in the sufferings of Israel in the exile there is foreshadowed the way in which God will redeem the world. The sin of the world is to be heaped upon Israel: and this weight, which Israel as a whole cannot bear, is to be heaped in turn upon Israel's representative, the King of the Jews. On the cross Jesus *is* Israel. He *is* the servant. He is obedient to the vocation to which Israel was called. The Messiah had not come to rule the world as a nationalist king, a rival to Caesar. He had come to rule the world as God always intended to have his world

34

ruled — by loving the world and dying for it. He had come to take the pain of the world on to himself, to draw it into his own being, to bend his back under the load that Israel and the world could not carry, to receive in the palms of his hands the nails of rough Roman justice, to have ringing in his ears the anger of frustrated Jewish hopes. He who would be greatest among you must be your servant.

It is these old promises, and this ancient vocation, to which Jesus is being obedient as he goes to Calvary. The doctrine of the atonement, which has puzzled so many scholars and theologians down the years, is not a matter of our arbitrarily attributing to the cross a significance which in and of itself it did not have, a sort of theory according to which God just decided to count the death of this one person as somehow effective to forgive sins which somehow could not otherwise be forgiven. Many people have rightly reacted against that sort of arbitrary, almost random picture of God's dealings with his world. No: in essence the biblical scheme of thought is richer and in fact ultimately simpler, integrating itself into five propositions:

(i) The world, and humans within it, are the good creation of the wise and loving God;

(ii) Humans have rebelled against their creator, and so are enslaved to the dark powers that rule the world;

(iii) God has set in motion a plan by which he himself can heal and restore humans and the whole cosmos, and this plan involves the calling of Israel; but Israel as a nation shares the plight of humanity, and so cannot accomplish that task as she stands;

(iv) God promises to send one who will do Israel's task, who will save Israel and the world, by dying on their behalf; this turns out in retrospect to be a promise which only the coming of God himself can fulfil;

(v) God promises that he will implement this act of salvation by sending his own Spirit to complete the healing and renewal of humankind and the whole cosmos.

And when, on the night he is to be betrayed, Jesus of Nazareth takes bread and breaks it and, adapting the words of the Passover service, the Jewish covenant festival, refers to his own forthcoming death; and when he describes the cup of wine as the new covenant, made in his blood for them and for many — there can be no doubt that he believed that these promises were coming true in and through his death. And when, in this whole context, the evangelists draw our attention to the title on the cross — the King of the Jews! — we can at last see in its full splendour the point they are making. Jesus on the cross is precisely — Jesus the representative King of the Jews! He is doing what Israel was called to do; Israel's task has devolved on to him, on to him alone. There was no other good enough to pay the price of sin; he only could unlock the gate of heaven, and let us in.

That is why it was impossible that the true Messiah should endorse or underwrite Israel's nationalist political ambitions. God never intended to fulfil his purposes that way. Israel politically and nationally could never be the means of saving the world. She needed saving herself. When John the Baptist preached to Israel (and it was of course in that context that Jesus received the dramatic confirmation of his own vocation) he warned them that the nation as a whole could not be God's instrument of salvation; that they too needed to repent, to seek God's salvation for their sin, because if they didn't there was judgment waiting.

And that became the keynote of Jesus' preaching as well. Like John, he warned continually of judgment to come. (We don't often stress this, but if you read quickly through the Gospels at one sitting, looking for this theme, you will be astonished how many warnings there are, on the lips of Jesus, about the awful disaster that Israel is courting by persisting in her present ways.) But the judgment of which he was speaking was not so much some kind of supernatural judgment after human death. Just like Jeremiah, warning the people that if they didn't repent God would judge them by bringing up the king of Babylon to attack Jerusalem, so Jesus warns Israel that if she does not repent God will use *Rome* as his instrument of wrath against his disobedient people. Rome, of course, didn't see it that way any more than Babylon had done six hundred years earlier. We are invited, by Jesus and the evangelists, to look at these pagan nations from God's point of view. And this is the point at which fear and trembling come upon us as we consider what it is that Jesus is saying.

On the one hand, he is saying that the wrath of Rome is going to descend upon Israel, and when it does it is to be understood as God's punishment of his rebellious people, twisting their national vocation into a demonic nationalist arrogance.

On the other hand, he is *identifying himself with* that sinful nation — with Zacchaeus, with Mary Magdalene, with Barabbas, with the moral and spiritual lepers as well as the physical ones, with those who were turning Israel's vocation into a nationalist dream; and in taking their identity on himself he goes to his death on a Roman cross, marked out as King of the Jews. If they do this when the wood is green, what will they do when it is dry? Jesus is dying the death of the nationalist rebel, the death he had predicted for the nation, though he alone was utterly innocent of that rebellion against God, or against Rome, which was the reason for the imminent judgment. He has gone in to eat with a man who is a sinner. He is numbered with the transgressors. On the cross Jesus, so to speak, becomes a zealot, a rebel, just as in that sense he became a sinner by eating with Zacchaeus, or became unclean when touched by the sick woman. What does this mean?

I believe that Jesus loved his people. It grieved him to see their oppression, with the poor all around him getting poorer, with one Jew turning against another Jew, and both of them hating the Romans. He felt keenly the hopes and ambitions of his people. His temptations were therefore real temptations. He felt the pain of seeing his fellow-Jews crushed under the pagan boot. He, like many others, was angry at the corruption of the life of the people under cynical pagan rulers and cynical Jewish quislings or power-politicians. He loved his people. He loved Jerusalem. When he predicted its destruction, he wasn't gloating. He was weeping. He would have loved to have been able to be her David in the way she wanted — to kill the giant, to set the people free. But he was mastered by a deeper love, a love that saw that political Messiahship would solve nothing. He loved his people — he loved the world — so deeply that half measures were out of the question. He could neither go to battle in the way she wanted nor retire to the sidelines. He had to hear the tempter out, to taste the cup to the dregs.

There is a strange parallel here with the old legend of Odysseus. He is on his way back from the Trojan war, sailing from one danger to another. And one of the dangers he has to pass is the island where the Sirens live, singing their song of intense beauty and exquisite though deadly power. Odysseus is warned that no man who hears it can resist it, and that all who obey the lure end up dead on the shore. So he has his men stop their ears with wax, and tie him, with his ears open, to the mast of the ship, with their only orders that if they perceive him trying to tell them to loose him they will tie him tighter. So Odysseus comes within sound of the Sirens' voices, and the strange longing surges through him, so that he is in an agony of desire to obey, to yield; and his deaf sailors, seeing him struggle to be free, simply tie him tighter. He experiences to the full the desperate agony of listening to the song and of being unable, through his own prior decision, to do what it bade him. I see him in my mind's eye tied there, his arms stretched out to either side, lashed to the crossbeam of the mast, with his overwhelming longing to yield to the lovely voice held firmly in check by his determination to remain obedient, a determination already effected in his orders to his men.

Jesus had no men to whom he could give such orders. The orders all came, and continued to come, from within himself. And so he hung there outside his beloved Jerusalem, having listened to the sweet song, the song of liberty, that she had been singing to him these many years, and having set his face against it by his own act of obedient will. And now, like Adam outside the garden, he looks on Jerusalem finally from beyond the walls, and loves her still, through obedient, dying eyes, taking on himself in his innocent love the judgment she had merited, becoming in very truth the King of the Jews. The cross is his enthronement as the Messiah of Israel, because there he finally does for Israel and the world what Israel's Messiah had to do, revealing in the process that all earthly kingdoms are as dust and ashes before the Kingdom of God.

Think of David, the man after God's own heart, going to meet Goliath, with five smooth stones taken from the brook, and defeating him in the name of the God of Israel. Now think of Adam, driven from the garden (which, according to Jewish and early Christian legend, was in the Jerusalem area, so that Adam was finally himself buried on the very spot where Jesus was crucified, which is why in paintings and stained-glass windows we see Adam's skull at the foot of the cross); think of Adam, now forced to eat bread in the sweat of his brow. Now put the two pictures, David and Adam, together, and look at them through the lens of Calvary itself.

> David, where are you? Off to meet the giant
> With four smooth nails I've taken from the wine-press.
> Adam, where are you? Here, outside the gate,
> The wrong side of the whirling, flaming sword:
> Loving you, golden Jerusalem, through obedient eyes,
> That in the blood of my brow you may eat bread.

Merciful God, you made all people, and you hate nothing that you have made; you do not desire the death of a sinner, but rather that he should be converted and live. Have mercy upon your ancient people, the Jews, and upon all who have not known you and your love in your son, the King of the Jews, or who deny or oppose the faith of the crucified Messiah; take from them all ignorance, hardness of heart, and contempt for your word, and so fetch them home to your fold, that they may be made one flock under one shepherd: through the same Jesus, the Messiah, our Lord and King. Amen.

6

'This man is calling Elijah.'

Now from the sixth hour there was darkness over all the land until the ninth hour. And about the ninth hour Jesus cried with a loud voice, 'Eli, Eli, lama sabachthani?', that is, 'My God, my God, why hast thou forsaken me?' And some of the bystanders hearing it said, 'This man is calling Elijah.' And one of them at once ran and took a sponge, filled it with vinegar, and put it on a reed, and gave it to him to drink. But the others said, 'Wait, let us see whether Ehjah will come to save him.' And Jesus cried again with a loud voice and yielded up his spirit. (Matthew 27.45-50 RSV)

One of the strangest of all the things said about Jesus as he hung on the cross is this response to his cry of agony. At about the ninth hour — what today we would call three o'clock in the afternoon — Jesus cried out with a loud voice, 'Eli, Eli, lama sabachthani?' Now we know, not least because the evangelists make it clear, that Jesus was quoting from Psalm 22, and that his words meant, 'My God, my God, why have you forsaken me?' or, 'why did you abandon me?' But some of the bystanders didn't hear it properly, or perhaps didn't understand the dialect

41

or accent in which Jesus spoke, with his voice coming out of his unimaginable physical agony. So, picking up his first words, they said, 'This man is calling Elijah.' And some said, 'Wait — let's see whether Elijah will come to save him.'

Now these odd comments are probably lost on most modern readers. But to the Jewish audience for whom Matthew, at least, was writing they would have had great significance.

What did the Jews believe about Elijah? Anyone who has been a guest, as I have two or three times, at a Jewish Passover meal, a Seder night, will know that, from very early times, there has been a tradition that the prophet Elijah will come back to deliver God's people, or perhaps to prepare the way for the messianic deliverer himself. On Passover night, you leave the door open for Elijah to come in. You put out a special cup of wine for Elijah to drink in case he should come. The feast will not be complete until God does for his people what they long and hope that he will do — until, that is, he sends his messenger to come and save them. And the Jewish people still express their longing that 'next year in Jerusalem' they will celebrate the true Passover in the finally redeemed Kingdom of God.

In the Dead Sea Scrolls this hope is turned into the idea of a priestly Messiah, who would be the companion, or perhaps the forerunner, of the royal Davidic Messiah. And among the Jews of Jesus' day there was a general, somewhat confused, expectation that Elijah would come and restore the world, or at least Israel, to its rightful order before the final ushering in of the Kingdom of God.

So what were the bystanders saying when they thought that Jesus on the cross was calling for Elijah? They were imagining, I think, that Jesus, too, was in the same state of longing and expectation that all Judaism was in. The Jews, living under the Roman oppression, were longing for God to act to deliver them. And in that week, which was the week of Passover, this hope would have explicitly included the coming of Elijah. These bystanders were probably going home that night to keep the passover themselves, to pour the cup of wine for Elijah, to leave the door open for him to come in. How natural, then, that they should see in Jesus the intensification and climax of their own anguish, as he, in agony on the cross which summed up all that the Roman oppression meant to Israel, cried out (as they thought) for Elijah to come and rescue him, for God to step in and end the torture of his people!

And who was this Elijah that they were longing for? He was the man of fire. He it was who called down fire to burn up the troops sent by the wicked king Ahaziah to fetch him. He it was who poured water on the sacrifice prepared as a contest between Yahweh, Israel's God, and Baal, the Canaanite fertility god, and then prayed for fire to come and burn up the sacrifice — and the fire of God fell, and burned up the sacrifice, and licked up the water that was in the trench. And he it was who went up to heaven with horses and a chariot of fire. And the watchword that Elijah gave to the people when they were drawing near for the great contest with the prophets of Baal was: 'The god who answers by fire — let him be God.' It was a man of fire that was wanted: someone who would purify and purge Israel, but who more especially would call down the divine fire upon the enemies of God's people.

And the disciples had hoped that Jesus would be Elijah. When John the Baptist pointed to Jesus he said that he would be the one to baptise with fire. James and John asked Jesus' permission to call down fire on those who rejected their message. It was only by a slow process that they came to the realisation that Jesus was more than a prophet — that he was actually the Messiah; that he was the King, not the herald. And when Elijah appeared talking with Jesus on the mountain of transfiguration, the disciples were astonished, and said, 'Why then do people say that Elijah must come first?' Jesus' reply indicated clearly enough that it was John the Baptist, not himself, who must be thought of as Elijah, the forerunner. But the confusion remained, as far as the crowds were concerned, right up to the end; and it comes out again now as Jesus hangs upon the cross.

Because Jesus was not, of course, calling for Elijah. The

misunderstanding of the crowds was a matter not just of language, but of theology. They were not merely mistaking the word 'Eli', 'my God', for 'Elijah': they were failing to realise the whole meaning of Jesus' life, and now of his death. Jesus has already gone beyond the point of Elijah's return: 'Elijah has already come,' he said to them on the mountain, 'and they did to him whatever they wanted.' John the Baptist had prepared Israel for the coming of the Messiah, and he had died at the hands of Herod's executioners. For Jesus, God's great act of redemption was no longer delaying: it was well under way, entering now its last and most bitter phase. On the night he was betrayed, Jesus celebrated the Passover with his disciples, and this time the cup meant for Elijah was passed round among the disciples: 'This cup,' said Jesus, 'is the new covenant in my blood.' Elijah's work is done. We come now to a new age, the age of the new covenant, the age of the forgiveness of sins. And the door of that Passover room opened, not to let Elijah in, but to let Judas out. Elijah has already come: and his ministry is now taken up in the ministry of Jesus himself, the King, the one whose way Elijah prepared. 'I shall not eat this passover again', he said, 'until it is fulfilled in the Kingdom of God; I shall not drink again of the fruit of the vine until the Kingdom of God comes.' When will that be? Next year in Jerusalem? No: next day outside Jerusalem. That was where the true Passover was to take place — the final great act of redemption in which the people would be set free, not from Egypt or Rome but from the great grim gaoler for whom Egypt, Babylon, and finally Rome were just pictures.

But how is the King achieving this? How is he delivering his people from their bondage? How is he being God's agent in the redemption and renewal of Israel and the world? What the crowds could not hear in the cry from the cross was the voice of desolation, of God-forsakenness, wrung from the very soul of one who was being wounded for their transgressions, not his own; bruised for their iniquities, not his own. Upon him was the punishment that brought them peace; with his stripes they were being healed. They, and we with them, were lost sheep without a shepherd:

and the Lord laid on him the iniquity of us all. And Jesus, in that hour, experienced the darkness and the horror from which he, even he, had shrunk in Gethsemane, from which not only Satan, not only Judas, not only Peter, but also all his natural inclinations, all his love of his own people, had done their best to turn him aside. In identifying totally with the sin of the world, he became cut off from the presence of God. At the very moment when he was most fully embodying the love of God, he found himself totally separated from the love of God, the love which he had known in precious intimacy ever since childhood.

This, then, was the end of the road which he had begun to tread in his baptism by John, the Elijah who had indeed come: identifying with sinners, so that sinners could be saved. This was where it had all led. The road ended not only in the bitterness of apparent failure, not only in the physical torment of a cruel and gruesome death, but in the spiritual darkness of separation from God, bearing upon himself the sins of the world. *That* is how the world was redeemed: not by Elijah and the Messiah coming and ridding Israel of her political foes, calling down fire to burn up all opposition, but by Jesus, commissioned by John in the spirit and power of Elijah, ridding Israel and the world of her true enemies. Just as Elijah challenged the powers of darkness to that great contest, in which the god who answered by fire was to be God, so now Jesus takes on the rulers of the world: the might of Rome, the law of Israel, and behind both the usurping and destroying power of Satan. And this time the rules of the contest are: the god who answers by love, let *him* be God.

Almighty God, from whom proceeds the fire of love which alone can destroy and purge all the evil of our hearts, and of our world: send your loving Holy Spirit upon your people, baptizing us again with that holy fire, that we may ourselves be delivered from the snares of the enemy and be liberated to bring your love and redemption to the ends of the world: through Jesus Christ our Lord. Amen.

7

'Truly, this man was the Son of God.'

And when the sixth hour had come, there was darkness over the whole land until the ninth hour. And at the ninth hour Jesus cried with a loud voice, 'Eloi, Eloi, lama sabachthani?' which means, 'My God, my God, why hast thou forsaken me?' And some of the bystanders hearing it said, 'Behold, he is calling Elijah.' And one ran and, filling a sponge full of vinegar, put it on a reed and gave it to him to drink, saying, 'Wait, let us see whether Elijah will come to take him down.' And Jesus uttered a loud cry, and breathed his last. And the curtain of the temple was torn in two, from top to bottom. And when the centurion, who stood facing him, saw that he thus breathed his last, he said, 'Truly this man was the Son of God!' (Mark 15.33-39 RSV)

Our final witness is another (at first sight) unlikely one. Like Pilate, he is a pagan, a Roman. Unlike Pilate the scheming politician, he is a seasoned, no doubt hard-bitten, Roman soldier. And his comment on Jesus' death is therefore all the more revealing, at the end of St Mark's account of the crucifixion. He watches Jesus die, and says, 'Truly, this man was the Son of God.'

The centurion had seen plenty of other executions before. Most likely in his time he had often enough hammered the nails, or held the victim while someone else was doing so. What did he see that was so special about this one? What on earth prompted him to say such a thing? And what significance does Mark intend it to have for his readers?

To understand this we need, I believe, to go back to Jesus' trial again: not, this time, his trial before Pilate, where he was arraigned on a trumped-up political charge of sedition, but to the more complex trial before Caiaphas the High Priest, where he was on a very different charge, namely, blasphemy. This trial, like so many things in the passion story, was the culmination of a constant stream of accusations and threats that began to buzz around Jesus' head from the very early days of his ministry. Who is this that claims to forgive sins? Who is this who heals people on the Sabbath? Who does he think he is, to abolish the Judaic food laws and the Pharisaic traditions with one magisterial state-ment? People had *died* for these laws within living and fresh memory. Who does he imagine himself to be, saying things like 'You have heard that it was said' (in the Old Testament), 'but I say unto you'? What right does he have to say that? He is claiming an authority and status which look suspiciously as though he is arrogating to himself a position appropriate for God and God only. This is serious.

And so, by the time Jesus arrived in Jerusalem on the first Palm Sunday, the crowds might be shouting Hosanna, but in what we would now call the smoke-filled rooms, plots were being hatched. John suggests that a sort of trial had already been held without Jesus even being there, and that Caiaphas, cynical and wily old politician that he was, had declared that it was better that one man should die rather than have the whole nation perish. And John's comment is: precisely so, though you, Caiaphas, don't see the point. Jesus, the innocent one, was drawing on to himself the holy wrath of God against human sin in general, so that human sinners like you and me can find, as we look at the cross, that the load of sin and guilt we have been carrying is taken away from us. Jesus takes it on himself, and somehow absorbs it, so that when we look back there is nothing there. Our sins have been dealt with, and we need never carry their burden again.

That is one of the powerful reasons why Easter must follow Good Friday. The sin which caused Jesus' death has been dealt with, and death can hold him no more. We look again at the cross, and there is nothing there: he is not dead, he has risen, and with that news there runs around the globe the message: The oppressor of our people has been defeated! Tell Zion, 'Your God is King!' Isaiah had imagined essentially the same message being taken hot-foot to Jerusalem at the end of the exile; now his prophecy is fulfilled in a richer sense still. This is not abstract theology, this is hard fact: the God who made promises to you, that there would be an end of the night of sin and suffering — this God has acted within his own world to take the sin and suffering on to himself and so bring it to an end, and now he has celebrated his triumph over it and wants the world to share the good news.

But all this raises for us, as Jesus' apparent claims did for Caiaphas, the question: Who *is* this? Caiaphas, in the trial, brought the issue to a head by asking Jesus, on oath, whether he was the Messiah, the Son of the Blessed One. Now please note: by itself that question is not necessarily a question about Jesus' divinity. The phrase 'Son of God' at this period of Judaism doesn't mean what it does in later Christian language. It refers to the Messiah, the anointed, but still merely human, king. Caiaphas is simply asking Jesus whether he thinks he is the Messiah, and the Jews did not believe in a divine Messiah *per se*. Caiaphas already knows the answer within in his own frame of reference: it is quite impossible, out of the question, that this strange, deluded, fanatical north-countryman should be the Lord's anointed. But Jesus, too, knows the answer from *his* point of view. 'I am,' he replies; 'and you, Caiaphas, will see the Son of Man sitting on the right hand of Power, and coming on the clouds of heaven.' If we

49

understand properly what is going on in the two passages of the Old Testament Jesus is there weaving together, we will not think of this strange and (to us) dark saying as a prediction that Caiaphas will see Jesus coming *down to earth* on the clouds of heaven. The Son of Man in Daniel's vision is the representative of Israel, who is vindicated by God, raised up to glory, after his suffering at the hands of the monsters who represent the enemies of God's people. Jesus is taking on himself the identity of the people of God, of Israel; Israel's destiny, to suffer and die under the weight of the world's sin, has now devolved on to him, but God will vindicate him when the job is done. Open your eyes, Caiaphas, he seems to be saying: you think you are trying me in your little court, but the real court scene is going on right now in heaven, and pretty soon I will be shown to be in the right, and you will thereby be shown to be in the wrong.

And when Jesus is vindicated the appropriate way of speaking of that great divine act is that he will be seated at the right hand of Power, and coming on the clouds of heaven. That is, he will share the very throne of God himself, will attain to a glory which is God's and only God's, and will attain it accompanied by those clouds which, always in the Old Testament, signal a revelation of God himself.

So it is that Jesus must answer Caiaphas with a 'yes', but with a qualified yes. He is Messiah, but his Messiahship is quite different from Caiaphas's ideas of it. For the High Priest, a lonely Messiah at the mercy of a court of law was a contradiction in terms, and he was about to prove his point by having him crucified. For Jesus, Messiahship meant precisely the loneliness, the misunderstanding, and the shameful death *by which the world was to be redeemed;* and he was about to demonstrate his point by going obediently to be crucified.

From this perspective we can at last return to the question we asked right at the beginning. On the cross, was Jesus a failed Messiah or a successful Messiah? The crowds mocked him and said, 'If you are the Messiah, come down from the cross, and we will believe in you.' But — precisely because he is the Messiah, he must stay on the cross. He is doing what only he can do. He is the sole, unique innocent one, bearing the pain, the shame, the guilt of the world. And if he were to come down from the cross now — if he were at this last moment to be disobedient to his unique vocation — the game would be over. Satan would have won after all. The world would not be redeemed. It is because he is the Son of God, and that in a deeper sense than Caiaphas could have imagined, that he must die on the cross, doing that which only the Son of God can do. Only so can the world be redeemed.

Caiaphas, then, was bound to regard Jesus' claims as blasphemy, but Jesus was in fact uttering the sober truth. To understand this we need to see it, once more, from the perspective of the Old Testament. There are several relevant passages, of which this is perhaps the most striking:

> I looked, but there was no one to help; I was appalled, but there was no one to uphold; so my own arm brought me victory, and my wrath upheld me. . . . I will recount the steadfast love of the Lord, the praises of the Lord, according to all that the Lord has granted us, and the great goodness to the house of Israel which he has granted them according to his mercy, according to the abundance of his steadfast love. For he said, Surely they are my people, sons who will not deal falsely; and he became their Saviour. In all their affliction he was afflicted, and the angel of his presence saved them; in his love and in his pity he redeemed them; he lifted them up and carried them all the days of old. (Isaiah 63.5, 7-9 RSV; compare Isaiah 59.15-16; Ezekiel 34.11-23)

God declares as he looks at the world of humankind that there is nobody who can stand outside the universal problem of sin and deal with it: and he concludes — therefore I will come, myself, and rescue them. The task of redeeming the world, to which Israel was called but of which she was incapable, and to which Israel's representative, the Davidic King, was called in her

51

place, was ultimately a task which only God himself could perform. Granted the fact of universal human sin, only God can be obedient to the saving plan, an innocent one who can absorb and deal with the sin of the world, taking the curses of the world and continuing to give back blessing, taking the hatred of the world and continuing to give back love.

Consider what happens normally in the world. When we are cursed, we curse back, if only in our hearts. When we are hated, we pass the hate on; we keep it, so to speak, in circulation. Someone is mean to me, so I take out my feelings on someone else, probably someone weaker than me. So it goes on — in the world of humankind. Tiberius Caesar, growing old and suspicious, is ever more likely to take it out on his government officials; and Pontius Pilate is afraid of what may happen when he gets back to Rome if reports circulate about his ham-handed administration. Pilate, in turn, takes out his fear and spite on the subject people who find themselves at his mercy. The Jews, meanwhile, have reasons enough of their own to be bitter and frustrated, and a would-be Messiah who doesn't deliver the goods is an ideal target; and so the weight of the world's insecurity, anger, bitterness, hostility, is heaped on to the head of Mary's son, the young man from Nazareth. 'Ah, holy Jesus, how hast thou offended, that Man to judge thee hath in hate pretended?'

But the divine way is different. Jesus takes temptation, hatred, curses — the bitterness of a bitter world — and he absorbs it into himself on the cross. Jesus, pronounced guilty as a blasphemer for claiming to be the Son of God, demonstrates on the cross that he was speaking the truth, by doing what only the Son of God could do — loving his own who were in the world, he loved them to the end, the bitter end. And this pattern, acted out uniquely on the cross, becomes then for us, by the Spirit of Jesus working within us, the pattern we are commanded to live out, as we give back good for evil, blessing for curse, prayer for persecution. One might say that this is *the* vocation of the Church: to take the sadness of the world and give back no anger; the sorrow of the world, and give back no bitterness; the pain of the

world, and not sink into self-pity; but to return forgiveness and
love, blessing and joy. That is what Jesus was doing on Calvary.
He drew on to himself the sin of the ages, the rebellion of the
world and humankind, the hatred, pain, anger, and frustration
of the world, so that the world and humankind might be healed,
might be rid of it all.

And the centurion, knowing the nature of the charge against
Jesus, looks on in awe and amazement and declares — 'So he
really *was* Son of God, after all.' Two days later, of course, God
is going to declare, powerfully, that Jesus really was innocent,
really was Son of God. But if we understand the cross we can see
that, to the eye of faith, the evidence is already there. Because on
the cross we see a love which is none other than God's own love.
Only God loves like that. Jesus said, 'Greater love has no man
than this, that a man lay down his life for his friends.' But on the
cross there was a greater love nailed up in public, when God gave
his life for his enemies. We cannot understand the cross unless
we understand the incarnation, and vice versa. As St Paul put it
— God was in Christ, reconciling the world to himself. The words
that Jesus himself spoke at supper on the night he was betrayed
are, as it were, magnified into the words that God himself says,
not with speech but with action, on the first Good Friday: 'This
is my body, broken for you.'

It is because in his death on the cross we see a love which
can only be identified as God's love that we Christians say: He
was not just a great teacher, dying for his beliefs. He was not just
a good man suffering innocently. He was, and is, the loving God
himself, come as a human being to save men, women, and children from sin and death, and from all the stain and fear and guilt
and shame which cling to our hearts, our memories, our imagi-
nations, our lives. People still puzzle over how Jesus can be divine
and human at the same time. It remains a puzzle if we assume
that the word 'God' refers to a distant, detached, supernatural
landlord. Many people still think the word 'God' refers to a being
like that. But try imagining the Old Testament God for a minute
— passionate, involved with his people in their wanderings and

stupidity, loving them tenderly and rescuing them again and again, grieving over their folly and their pain, taking costly action to redeem them. What would *that* God look like if he were to become human, and live among us humans? I think he would look very much like Jesus of Nazareth; and never more so than as he hangs dying on the cross.

And, in Mark's Gospel, written quite likely for a Roman audience, the centurion's comment implicitly asks the question: Have you stood before the cross and recognised that here there is an act of love which marks out this man as none other than the Son of God? Have you allowed yourself to accept what was there accomplished on your behalf? Do you still, like so many, regard Good Friday as an awkward, somewhat embarrassing moment, stuck between the Hosannas of Palm Sunday and the Hallelujahs of Easter Day? Or have you learnt to recognise that, on Calvary, Jesus — even through his fear, his doubts, his final bitter temptations — was completing the obedient vocation he had undertaken? And have you attempted to bring the pains and puzzles and tragedies of your own life into the searching, but amazingly loving, light of that cross? If you have, you may have begun to realise this great truth: that here we cannot reduce the cross to either an abstract idea of 'atonement', or to a set of 'bare historical facts.' Instead, the cross itself summons us to rethink and remake the whole fact and idea of knowledge itself, belief itself, life itself. Here we are unmade; here we are remade.

Two great classics, in different spheres, draw the threads together. In Bach's *St Matthew Passion,* towards the close, the centurion's words ('Truly, this was the Son of God') are given not to a soloist, as you might expect, but to the whole chorus, singing softly and penitently. They are not in the key one might expect for soloist or chorus, but are transposed into the key normally reserved for Christ himself. And into the bass line Bach has woven the musical letters which represent his own name. That, I suggest, is a true reading and re-presentation of the centurion's words. They are the response of the awed and grateful people of God to this all-but-unbelievable revelation of love; and within that response we are, each of us, to write our names into the chorus. And the key in which we sing is not our own, a merely human key: it is the key which conforms, as now at last because of the cross and the Spirit we can conform, to the initiating sovereign love of God in Christ. He has been singing his own song to his people all this time; and now, because of his death, we are at last able to respond in the same key. Truly, we say, this man dying for us is the Son of God. On the cross we see dying love, and we recognise it as the undying love of God.

Now I cannot know what burdens may be carried by those who read this book. I do know, because I know it for myself, that the sight of the cross can ease those burdens. That is the picture in my second classic text, Bunyan's *Pilgrim's Progress*, where Bunyan's Christian is trudging along, carrying his enormous load of sin and guilt on his shoulders. Bunyan writes, in words which need no further comment, that Christian

> came to a place where there stood a Cross, and, a little below, a sepulchre. So I saw in my dream, that just as Christian came up with the cross, his Burden loosed from off his shoulders, and fell from off his back, and began to tumble, and so continued to do, till it came to the mouth of the sepulchre, where it fell in, and I saw it no more. Then was Christian glad, and said with a merry heart: 'He hath given me rest by his sorrow, and life by his death.'

Almighty God, you have revealed yourself, in the cross of Jesus Christ, to be our God; to be a God of infinite and tender love. Open our eyes afresh, that we may see your dying love and respond to it from the depths of our hearts; and, responding, may find that the way of the cross is indeed for us too the way of truth and peace and life: through the same Jesus Christ, your Son, our Lord. Amen.

PART TWO

THE FIRE OF LOVE

8

The New Creation

After these things Jesus showed himself again to the disciples by the Sea of Tiberias; and he showed himself in this way. Gathered there together were Simon Peter, Thomas called the Twin, Nathanael of Cana in Galilee, the sons of Zebedee, and two others of his disciples. Simon Peter said to them, 'I am going fishing.' They said to him, 'We will go with you.' They went out and got into the boat, but that night they caught nothing.

Just after daybreak, Jesus stood on the beach; but the disciples did not know that it was Jesus. Jesus said to them, 'Children, you have no fish, have you?' They answered him, 'No.' He said to them, 'Cast the net to the right side of the boat, and you will find some.' So they cast it, and now they were not able to haul it in because there were so many fish. That disciple whom Jesus loved said to Peter, 'It is the Lord!' When Simon Peter heard that it was the Lord, he put on some clothes, for he was naked, and jumped into the sea. But the other disciples came in the boat, dragging the net full of fish, for they were not far from the land, only about a hundred yards off.

When they had gone ashore, they saw a charcoal fire there, with fish on it, and bread. Jesus said to them, 'Bring some of the fish that you have just caught.' So Simon Peter went aboard and hauled the net ashore, full of large fish, a hundred and fifty-three of them; and though there were so many, the net was not torn. Jesus said to them, 'Come and have breakfast.' Now none of the disciples dared to ask him, 'Who are you?' because they knew it was the Lord. Jesus came and took the bread and gave it to them, and did the same with the fish. This was now the third time that Jesus appeared to the disciples after he was raised from the dead.

When they had finished breakfast, Jesus said to Simon Peter, 'Simon son of John, do you love me more than these?' He said to him, 'Yes, Lord; you know that I love you.' Jesus said to him, 'Feed my lambs.' A second time he said to him, 'Simon son of John, do you love me?' He said to him, 'Yes, Lord; you know that I love you.' Jesus said to him, 'Tend my sheep.' He said to him the third time, 'Simon son of John, do you love me?' Peter felt hurt because he said to him the third time, 'Do you love me?' And he said to him, 'Lord, you know everything; you know that I love you.' Jesus said to him, 'Feed my sheep. Very truly, I tell you, when you were younger, you used to fasten your own belt and to go wherever you wished. But when you grow old, you will stretch out your hands, and someone else will fasten a belt around you and take you where you do not wish to go.' (He said this to indicate the kind of death by which he would glorify God.) After this he said to him, 'Follow me.' (John 21.1-19 NRSV)

We stood in the sunshine at the foot of the Mount of Olives, and looked at the garden of Gethsemane beside us and the Temple Mount opposite us.

'Tell me', I said. 'Don't you find it amazing to think of Jesus kneeling here, deciding to go up there and die for the sins of the world?'

'I find it difficult to believe that,' came the reply.

'Can't you believe that at least that's what *he* thought?' I said. 'After all, isn't it possible that he had figured out that he was called to be what Israel had been called to be — the light of the world — and that he had realised that this meant going and dying on a cross?'

'Yes', came the reply. 'I guess I can believe that he thought of it like that. But I can't believe that it was actually true.'

'Why not?' I asked, being a glutton for punishment.

'Because the world has not changed,' came the reply. 'If he died to make it a good place, he didn't succeed. Two thousand years is a long time to wait for things to get better.'

And I looked up the Kidron valley this way and that, and I thought of what I had seen and heard in the three weeks I had been in Jerusalem at that stage. I thought of the settlements and the refugee camps. I thought of the beggars in the streets and the taxi that wouldn't take me where I wanted to go because the driver was afraid of that part of town. I thought of the unexplained explosions, of the hatred in newspaper articles and the contempt in the eyes of policemen. I wanted to say, 'What about St Francis?', and then I thought of the arrogance of the monks in the church of the Holy Sepulchre. I wanted to say, 'What about Mother Teresa?', and then I thought of the Crusades. I thought of a lot more, too, but I didn't find a quick reply come readily to mind.

Nor did I particularly want to. Because if there is an answer to that challenge it won't come simply in words. It will come in flesh and blood. The word became flesh, said St John, and the Church has turned the flesh back into words: words of good advice, words of comfort, words of wisdom and encouragement, yes, but what changes the world is flesh, words with skin on them, words that hug you and cry with you and play with you and love you and rebuke you and build houses with you and teach your children in school.

But I mustn't go too fast. I want to look at John 21. It is all about the strange glory and the glorious strangeness of the resurrection, and it seems to me that somewhere in there is

61

an answer, or the beginnings of an answer, to the question my friend raised in Gethsemane. How can we claim that on the cross the evil of the world has been dealt with? This chapter speaks powerfully about the newness of God's love, about freshness, about hope and new starts, about the tears that come when pain is shot through with joy.

The first thing is *new creation*. It is impossible to read John 21 and not feel the power of this theme. John writes it so artlessly, but it takes your breath away to read it. Here are the disciples — Peter and half a dozen of the others. The old gang. They've gone back to their fishing boat. I always find this a bit puzzling, and I'm never quite sure whether they were puzzled too, wondering whether they were supposed to go back to the old life; or whether this was just a one-off trip for old time's sake. Maybe they didn't know either. Quite often we do things and we don't know why, and part of the miracle is that God meets us there anyway. But there they are, working hard all night and getting nowhere slowly. You can feel the tiredness and the darkness and the frustration and perhaps the tetchiness between tired men on a dark night in a cold boat.

Then feel how John does it. 'Just after daybreak, Jesus stood on the beach.' Perhaps you've been up at sunrise by Tiberias or Capernaum and you can see it in your mind's eye: first a grey light, then brown, then a deep rich blue, then gold and a lighter blue, then all together and redder by the minute until the sun is finally up. You'd pay good money to see something like that if it only happened once a year and you had to queue to get in, but we take it for granted. John doesn't; he knows what he's doing. The disciples have already tasted the new creation, but they are struggling along at the moment in the darkness of the old creation. But with Jesus standing on the shore a new day is breaking. And he tells them where to cast the net. And they, the old professional fishermen, are too tired to disobey, and they get more fish in one cast than in the whole night long. And then — sense the newness about it all — it all happens at once. A quick comment, a wild look, grab a cloak, into the water, powerful strokes (though I suspect not very stylish), Peter makes it to the beach, the others bring the boat and the fish. It's Jesus! It's Jesus! and he tells them to bring some of the fish, and to come and have breakfast.

John has put into story form the first, and in some ways the most important, thing that I want to say at this stage. We have got sidetracked in Western Christianity, I think, when we talk about the resurrection. We have got hung up about the physical facts of what happened on Easter morning — vitally important though that is — and when it comes to the *meaning* of the resurrection we go a bit flat. We talk about our own life after death and the fact that the resurrection guarantees that. Well, again, so it does. That's fine. But the resurrection means so much more than just what's going to happen to me and my body after I'm dead. I'm quite interested in what happens to me after I'm dead, but I'm not the only pebble on the beach, and the beach is more than the sum total of all the pebbles. The resurrection says not just that Jesus is alive today, and I can have a personal relationship with him — though that's true; not just that there is a life after death and I can enjoy it when I get there — though that's true too; the resurrection says that there is a *new world,* a new creation, a new order of being that has come into existence. God has made a way through death and out the other side, and the world as we know it — the world of beautiful sunrises and battered children, the world that gives us so much joy and pain in large doses — this world is itself, in and through that process, being put to death and brought through the grave to new life the other side.

The whole point about the resurrection, seen from this angle, is that the risen Jesus is the beginning of God's new world order, 'the firstfruits of those who slept.' He is the guarantee that love is stronger than death, that the God who made the world, and has grieved over its fall into sin and corruption, has not left it to stew in its own juice but has entered it, taken its pain and shame and death on to himself, and broken through to a new creation the other side. And this means that we are invited to look at the world in a whole new way. We are summoned to see everything — from fishing boats to frogspawn, from rainbows to refugee

camps — in a new way. We are summoned to let the morning
sun rise on our perceptions of God's world, to stop looking at
things the old way, blundering along in the dark, wondering why
we aren't catching any fish to speak of. We are invited to open
our eyes and see new life, open our minds and believe new life,
open our hearts and love new life, open our hands and *give* new
life. And we are invited to do this because Jesus is risen, and with
him new creation has come into being.

Now that's all very well. I suspect that my sceptical friend
wouldn't yet feel that due answer had been made. But it's a start,
and frankly a very necessary start. But John doesn't leave us there.
The scene moves in to the breakfast party on the shore. In the
Middle East a meal isn't the kind of couldn't-care-less affair it
sometimes is in some other cultures. It's an important occasion.
You belong to each other in a new way when you've eaten a meal
together. And Jesus seems to have spent a fair amount of time
eating with people — people of all sorts — during his ministry.
It wasn't just that of course he had to eat somewhere, and because
he was always on the move it tended to be with different people.
No: wherever he went, there was a party. There was a celebration.

And it all had to do with this old Jewish idea that when the
Messiah came there would be a great feast — the Messianic Banquet. The Messiah would sit down at table, and the true people
of Israel would sit and eat with him. They would be bound
together as God's people, and would celebrate the fact that Israel's
time of redemption had come at last. That's what Jesus was doing
all through his ministry, though it was always tinged with a dark
shadow because of the cross that was to come. And on the night
he was betrayed he celebrated the meal to end all meals — a
Passover with a difference, a liberation meal that ended in execu-
tion, a meal of triumph that pointed to tragedy. But now, on the
shore, in the early morning light, with Peter dripping wet and
feeling a bit foolish, and the others puffing up the beach dragging
the net, Jesus has made breakfast for them, and invites them to
share it with him. In the setting of new creation, Jesus is inviting
them to a *new celebration*. It is like the old meals he used to have

with them, except that now the dark shadow of the cross has been turned into the light of a new day. It's a celebration all right. There probably wasn't any dancing and singing, partly because they'd been fishing all night but partly, and more importantly, because there is such a thing as a joy that goes deeper even than dancing and singing, and I think that's what the disciples had that morning.

And we are called to join in that celebration. Not just for our own sakes, because Jesus wants us to feel good inside ourselves, though we will do so, as often as not, if we accept the invitation. Rather, because by joining in his meal, we become bonded to him, so that his new-creation life starts to become ours, not overnight most likely, but slowly and surely. If you want an example, look at the difference between Peter on the night he denied Jesus and Peter a few weeks later, standing before the rulers in Jerusalem and telling them, if you please, that he'd rather obey God than them. How had he got like that? By the new celebration of the new creation. The meals with Jesus and in commemoration of Jesus, the abiding presence of Jesus himself, had changed him and were changing him. When we celebrate Jesus' meal we aren't just whistling in the dark. Bread and wine are taken up in the Eucharist into God's future purposes, and become to us vehicles through which we can taste the fact that there is a new world, there is new hope, there is a new way to live and we are part of it. And our brokenness and tiredness, our crassness about the fish we haven't caught, and the long hours we have wasted doing our own thing instead of God's thing, somehow fall away, and we become people of the new celebration, people of the new creation, people of God's new world, which is a world of fresh light, fresh forgiveness, new starts, new hopes. We must learn to celebrate the fact that Christ is risen, and that — puzzled though we may still be about it — we are risen with him.

But my friend, I think, has still not received a full answer. If we leave it at that, the resurrection simply calls into being a private party, a Christian club, where we celebrate God's bright new world and look forward to full enjoyment of its benefits for ourselves — and leave the present world unchanged. There are many Christians who are in principle like that, for whom Jesus lived and died and rose again simply so that they individually would be all right eventually. That's not a bad place to start, but it's a sad place to end. Because when breakfast is finished, Jesus takes Peter for a long walk along the beach, and with the new creation light now higher in the sky, and the new celebration meal over, he talks to him about the *new commission* which must always follow.

Peter, you remember, had denied Jesus three times, just a short while before. Peter, who was going to be the great hero, waving his sword around like a blundering idiot in the garden, then lying and swearing because of a question from a servant-girl. My guess is that by the time Peter arrived at the shore, never mind by the time they had finished the meal, Peter knew there were things that had to be said. And there were. Three times Jesus asks him: 'Simon, son of John' (notice he doesn't call him Peter: he hadn't been very rock-like just then), 'do you love me more than these?' 'Simon, son of John, do you love me?' 'Simon, son of John, do you love me?' And you can perhaps feel the heart-breaking sense, not just of knowing you had completely and utterly let Jesus down, but also of realising that he had completely and utterly forgiven you, and was now standing there with love and new creation and healing in his face and his voice. And Peter says, three times: 'Yes, Lord, you know that I love you.'

And now comes the moment of the new commission. 'Peter, there is work for you to do. You're going to leave the fish business, which you know so much about; you're going to leave it for good, and you're going into the sheep business instead, which at the moment you know precious little about. I want you to feed my lambs. I want you to look after my sheep. I want to you feed my sheep. I want you to be you, because I love you and I have redeemed you; and I want you to work for me, because out there there are other people that I love, and I want you to be my word-become-flesh, my love sitting with them, praying with them, crying with them, celebrating with them. And how can you do it? By coming the way I came. You'll have to suffer a lot, because you will have to share the pain of the world if the world is to be healed through you, through me-in-you. You'll have to learn to listen to the pain of the world, to hear its silent crying as well as its strident and angry crying, and it will break your heart day by day as it broke mine. But I have sheep out there, and they need feeding, Peter, and I want you to do it for me. And don't worry about knowing how to go about it. All you have to do is follow me.'

And this is the answer that I hear in John's Gospel, the answer to my friend's question as to how Jesus' death is to change the world. It won't happen overnight — though actually a lot more *has* changed in two thousand years than we often remember. There are the St Francises and the Mother Teresas, and they matter. There are the Dietrich Bonhoeffers and the Janani Luwums, and we mustn't imagine that they were simply freaks. But a lot more still has to happen, even granted the fact that the world will only be totally healed when it is totally reborn. But God is calling Peters in every generation — calling people who have perhaps made a bit of a mess of things up till now, but whom Jesus is looking at with love and new creation and healing and inviting them to celebrate with him, and then to work with him and for him, that his sheep may be fed and that his world may be healed. Because there is more work still to be done, and we who breakfast with Jesus today must be prepared first for the long walk on the shore and then for the still longer walk to follow Jesus wherever he leads.

We cannot privatise the message of the resurrection. If it is good news for us, it is good news for the world. Without the new commission, the celebration can turn into a selfish indulgence, just as without the celebration the commission can be simply fishing in the dark, mere do-goodery that panders to our own pride or simply inflicts upon others our guilts or our fears. We are called to work under Jesus' direction: to catch more fish than we thought possible, and still find that the nets won't break, to learn from scratch how to feed sheep under his direction, and above all to follow him in the way of the cross, the way that shares and bears the pain of the world, the way that goes from Gethsemane up to the Temple Mount and then on again, up to the hill on the far side of the city, where the question of Gethsemane is finally answered. But the answer remains ultimately incomplete until it is worked out through Peter, and through you and me.

Jesus commissions us, then, to follow him: to where the hungry sit on the ground with distended stomachs; to where the dispossessed lie on the ground, past anger and past hope; to where the old people are forgotten, and the young people brutalised, where innocent villagers have their legs smashed with clubs and innocent passersby get blown up in car bombs. 'Follow me,' he says: 'to where the rich people buy unhappiness in expensive wrapping-paper, to where the poor people fight for the crumbs that the rich drop by accident; follow me, to where the religious people are using their religion as a screen to shut out the pain of the world, to where the unbelieving people are using the world as a screen to shut out the pain of God; follow me, to the villages and the towns, to the squatters' camps and the refugee compounds, to the bright lights of the city and the sad darkness of the depopulated countryside, to the corridors of power and the alleyways of despair, to the married people who have forgotten how to love and the unmarried people who long for the chance to learn how, to the businessman and the prostitute, the cameldriver and the taxi driver, the security force officers and the little boys throwing stones at them. Follow me: and tell them that I love them; tell them that I died for them; tell them I am alive for them; tell them that there is a new creation; tell them that there is a new celebration; tell them that there is a God who made them and yearns for them, and that if they find me they will find him.

'But, Peter, don't just tell them in words. Turn the words into flesh once more. Tell them by the marks of the nails in *your* hands. Tell them by your silent sharing of their grief, by your powerful and risky advocacy of them when they have nobody else to speak up for them. Tell them by giving up your life for them, so that when they find you they will find me. And Peter, remember: follow me.' And we are to follow him in the knowledge that the creation has been renewed, is being renewed, and one day will be renewed, until we sing together the song of the redeemed of the Lamb, the song of new creation and new celebration:

> I heard every creature in heaven and on earth and under the earth and in the sea and all therein, saying, 'To him who sits upon the throne and to the Lamb be blessing and honour and glory and might for ever and ever!' (Revelation 5.13 RSV)

Our calling is to say 'Amen' to that song, that vision, that hope; and to say it with word and with flesh, so that God the Father may be glorified, that God the Son may be satisfied, that God the Holy Spirit may be poured out upon us and upon the whole world.

Almighty Father, give us such faith in the risen and healing power of your Son, Jesus our Lord, that we may gladly and readily follow wherever he leads us, and embrace for his sake whatever tasks he entrusts to us, so that your sheep may be fed, and your world healed. We ask this through Jesus Christ, your Son, our Lord. Amen.

9

The Call of God

Now the Lord said to Abram, 'Go from your country and your kindred and your father's house to the land that I will show you. I will make of you a great nation, and I will bless you, and make your name great, so that you will be a blessing. I will bless those who bless you, and the one who curses you I will curse; and in you all the families of the earth shall be blessed.'

So Abram went, as the Lord had told him; and Lot went with him. Abram was seventy-five years old when he departed from Haran . . . and they set forth to go to the land of Canaan. (Genesis 12.1-5 NRSV)

As Jesus passed along the Sea of Galilee, he saw Simon and his brother Andrew casting a net into the sea — for they were fishermen. And Jesus said to them, 'Follow me and I will make you fish for people.' And immediately they left their nets and followed him. As he went a little farther, he saw James son of Zebedee and his brother John, who were in their boat mending the nets. Immediately he called them; and they left their father Zebedee in the boat with the hired men, and followed him. (Mark 1.16-20 NRSV)

71

There is a standard romantic tradition of how the call of God comes to a person. We envisage the lonely individual, out one night meditating under the stars, hearing a voice out of nowhere that challenges him (it's usually a him) to a new vocation. He takes it to be the voice of God, he sets off on his travels, and from then on works flat out for God through thick and thin.

And there are various passages in the Bible which really seem to reinforce that tradition. The call of Isaiah, for example — a vision of God in the temple, finishing up with, 'Whom shall I send?' 'Here am I, send me.' The call of the boy Samuel: 'Speak, Lord, thy servant heareth.' Paul on the road to Damascus. Peter, James, and John in the fishing boats. And, perhaps above all, the call of Abraham, at the end of the beginning of Genesis. In the beginning God created the heavens and the earth, and humans in his own image; his human creatures rebelled, Cain murdered Abel, the flood destroyed all except Noah and the chosen animals, and even after that they built the tower of Babel. Chaos, arrogance, sin, and death; and out of the midst of it God called Abraham to set about the long process of reversing the rebellion, called him to the lonely task of founding the family through whom the world would be put to rights again.

Now in a sense this tradition gives a true picture. There are moments when each individual stands alone before his or her maker, and business must be done on a strictly one-to-one basis, without fudging or sliding round the real issues. That can't be shirked. But I suspect that we rather enjoy the romantic tradition of the lonely individual hearing the voice of God and going off at once to obey, because it's so remote from our own experience that we don't feel either threatened or challenged by it. It's like a Superman movie: we watch the hero in amazement and awe, we get a spurious and vicarious enjoyment and feeling of satisfaction at his achievements (again, it's usually 'his'), and then go home feeling better but without any real personal engagement. And is that really it?

Let's flesh out the tradition a little bit. Abraham grew up in one of the best-known university towns of his day. It was a centre of learning and culture. The world was at his feet. He came from a good and respected family. They had lots of possessions, including a large household. Abraham had a position in society. He was established, a married and wealthy man. Abraham was the centre of a network of relationships, each one important, all together complex. He is no lonely romantic individual; even when he stands out under the stars and converses with God, it is Abraham the real human, not the idealised individual, who is doing business with his maker. And his maker tells him that he is to be involved in a different business from now on. He's got to get up and go — with his wife and household and flocks and herds, which is by itself something of a major operation if you think about it — to a country he's never visited, to attempt a task he's never thought of before. And we don't read that this happened in an instant. My guess is that Abraham had been aware of niggling feelings over a period of time, a growing unsettledness, a sense that there must be something more that he's meant to be doing. And as he tunes in to these voices within him, he learns bit by bit to recognize a sense of direction struggling to articulation. And when it reaches that point, he realises that the voice, though it assuredly sounds within his own imagination, is the voice of the creator God.

How can you tell it's the voice of God? That's a good question, and I suspect it was often as much a question for Abraham as it is for us. The fact that he's called the friend of God doesn't mean that it was any easier for him discerning what God was saying than it is for us, and sometimes, from the story, we have to conclude frankly that he misheard, misread the signals, got his wires thoroughly crossed. But part of the good news of the story is that this didn't seem to matter in the long term. The creator's voice was still to be heard — and you can tell it's he, ultimately, because what he's talking about is precisely the restoration and renewal *of* his creation. 'Abraham — up until now the human race has been lurching like a bunch of lemmings towards the cliff; arrogance, chaos, rebellion, despair, and the world itself, the beautiful created order, is out of control because its keeper, its steward, has abandoned his task. But now, Abraham, I am calling you to take up the position of responsibility which Adam vacated. I want you to begin the family — the one, unique family — through whom all the scattered families of the earth will be drawn together into one, reversing the tragedy of Babel. I want you to be my friend, so that the world may be healed.' And Abraham — not the lonely romantic dreamer but the shrewd middle-eastern bargainer, with his flocks and his herds and everything but the kitchen sink, gets up and goes.

It's an ambiguous journey, which later historians are perfectly free to classify as one more migration among the nomadic peoples of the area, and later sceptics are perfectly free to see as a self-interested search for fresh fields and pastures new. Abraham's family didn't march along carrying a banner saying 'We are the newly founded people of God.' They came when they were called (more or less); they went where they were sent (well, more or less); and they did what they were told (at least, some of the time). When we get inside the story, between Genesis 12 and 25, we find an ambiguity and an uncertainty which look a lot less like the romantic hero and a lot more like ordinary mortals. It may make a worse Superman comic-strip, but it certainly makes a better start to the story of the people of God. And if it makes it potentially more uncomfortable for us, I guess we have to be ready for that.

Because the call of God moves on. Abraham's family isn't founded in order that humans can from now on be absolved of their responsibility to listen, to choose, to act wisely in the world. It is founded in order to set humans free to do those things, and by doing them to set others free in turn to do them, and so in turn to set the world free to be God's world again. The promised land is to become the sign of a whole new world order. So God calls his people Israel, in the hauntingly beautiful series of pro-phetic voices that echo through the Old Testament — calls them to continue the Abrahamic task of being his people for the sake of the world. And Israel is of course as deeply ambiguous as Abraham, only if anything more so. She is surrounded by so many voices that she often seems to drift this way and that, pursuing now this call and now that one, sometimes hoping that she's following the voice of her God and sometimes perhaps hoping that she can, like Jonah, manage to escape it. The story of Israel can be romanticised too, as in some children's Bibles; but in the real Bible it certainly isn't. It's a messy story of a muddled people, making false moves and taking wrong turns, but always to their own surprise being brought back on track just when all seemed hopeless. But as the night got darker and darker, as Israel thought she was so stuck in persecution and so squashed by foreign oppression and so sick and tired of trying to find the way forward that many people were simply giving up on the whole thing, the strange thing happened again. We move forward in history to what we call the first century BC.

And again it is ambiguous. Israel is being narrowed down to a point, and there are those in Israel who are waiting and longing for God to act — and perhaps in many a Jewish girl's heart there is the dream that she is to be the mother of the Messiah. And then in one Jewish girl's heart there grows the belief that maybe after all it's going to be her; she battles with the fear, perhaps, that it's wishful thinking; she tells herself off for being silly; but the hope and belief grows and grows until one day it bursts into light and stands before her, her dream turned into flame and addressing her. And of course she says yes. But we mustn't imagine that Mary was a heroine, an Annie-get-your-gun type, grasping the promise of God and riding off with it through all the problems to emerge in triumph at the end. As we saw in an earlier chapter, she must lose her dream before she realises it. She must watch her Son, whom she thought was to be Messiah, taking up with the shabby crowd down at the pub. She must watch him being fawned over by the girls of the street, and not seeming to mind. And she must watch as his Messiahship is conclusively disproved as the occupying forces execute him as a failed Messiah, a would-be national leader who lets the people down. There is the obverse of the dramatic call of God. When God calls a woman, he bids her come and die — die to the hope she cherished, the hope she suckled, the hope born from her own womb and heart. Mary had been called to an ambiguous task — to have people up the street sneer at her, pregnant just a bit too soon, to have her pride and joy going off in quest of a Messiahship totally unlike her idea of Messiahship, to have him executed before her eyes. The call of God is not to become the heroine or hero in God's new Superman story. It is to share and bear the pain of the world, that the world may be healed.

And that is where the story opens up and becomes, if we will, our story. Because when Jesus comes into Galilee, preaching the gospel of the Kingdom of God, the first thing he does is to issue a call which is remarkably like God's call to Abraham. Remember how it ran? 'Leave your country and your father's house, and go to the place I will show you, and I will make of you a great nation.' Now it sounds like this: 'Leave your business, your father's workplace, and come with me; and I will give you another job to do, a job which will stretch you in new ways, draw out of you potential you never knew you had.' Again, we mustn't imagine that this call came out of the blue. There had been messianic rumblings and nationalist stirrings in Palestine for some while by the time Jesus arrived on the beach at Capernaum that day, and we can be pretty sure that Peter, James, and John were ready to go, taking a couple of swords with them. They were the sort who would want to — who would resent having to pay hard-earned money in taxes to the Romans, who would long to be able to bring up their own children in a free country, who might even, if they thought about it long enough, want to have the freedom to worship Israel's God with more leisure and study — though I'm not sure about the study, at least for Peter and James. Their motives, as becomes abundantly clear throughout the rest of the Gospel story, were pretty thoroughly mixed, and the mixture was not exactly fifty-fifty good and bad, either. And yet they obeyed: the oddest little raggle-taggle of nonheroes you ever saw, a kind of junior Dad's Army, with homegrown zeal and homespun philosophy. Hardly the sort to set the Jordan on fire; but that wasn't the intention. They were the ones who were going to be set on fire. When God calls a man, he bids him come and burn — burn with a new love, a new desire, that will take all the mixed and muddled desires and ambitions and burn till it has refined all that was God-given in them and purged out all that was going in the other direction.

> O let it freely burn,
> Till earthly passions turn
> To dust and ashes in its heat consuming.

That is the destiny of those whom God calls: to be 'consumed by either fire or fire', and in fact by both at once.

And it was this motley crew, this mixture of obedience and disobedience, this apology for a new people of God, who had their hopes shattered in turn when Jesus went to Jerusalem to die instead of swooping down on it like Superman, and who all ran away when the crunch came — this bunch of shreds and patches that became the people through whom, initially, the promise to Abraham began to be fulfilled, as they went out into all the world to bring healing and reconciliation and life and love, in the power and the fire of the Holy Spirit. God's call is not designed to make us supermen and superwoman, because that's not what the world needs; it needs men and women who are humble enough, and often that means humbled enough, to work from within, from below, not to impose a solution on the world from a great height but to live within the world as it is, allowing the ambiguities and the perplexities of their own sense or absence of vocation to be nevertheless the place where they listen for the voice of God, and struggle to obey as best they can. And the one place where Jesus said we could be sure of hearing the voice of God, his own voice, is in the cry of those in need — in physical, emotional, intellectual and spiritual need; the voice of the Spirit who is groaning within the pains of the world, the voice of the God who calls us not to impinge on the world with a new programme of do-goodery but to be his feet, his hands — and remember what happened to his hands — his healing touch, his tears, yes, and his laughter too, within the midst of his world. We are to be ourselves, yes, with all our background, all the lives that our lives touch, all the ambiguities that we carry about with us; but with all of these strangely transformed and taken up into the purposes of his love.

And we don't have to feel guilty if we aren't supermen or superwomen; we should feel guilty if we thought we were. Nor should we mind if we don't experience the great romantic thing of standing out under the stars and hearing God's voice (though it still does happen from time to time, and it's still ambiguous and puzzling when it does). Most people don't; most Christians don't; and that's normal and all right. What we must be doing, each one of us as individuals and us all together as a community, and indeed us as members of the many different wider communities which our lives touch, not least our own country at this moment in history — what we must be doing is to be listening, *within* the conflicting voices going on in our heads and our newspapers, our ambitions and our secret longings, listening for the genuine voice of our creator and lover, listening and ready to obey. And as we listen for the voice of the one who comes, we will perhaps recognise it if we maintain the balance between the song of the angels which we bear at Christmas and the songs of Passiontide which follow a few months later. We are to be neither triumphalists nor nihilists, neither arrogant nor despondent.

And if that balance is maintained we may perhaps be able to hear the voice which calls someone to follow Jesus for the first time ever; which calls someone else to leave this country as soon as may be and work their heart out to bring healing to a country far poorer than we can imagine; which calls someone else to spend long, hard years in training for medical or psychiatric work; someone else to look after handicapped children; someone else to enter the ambiguous sphere of politics; someone else to offer himself or herself for ordination, to preach the gospel and celebrate the sacraments. And in and through it all, we may hear the voice of God calling us to be wise and gentle in all our relationships; to be sensitive and forgiving, creative and sustaining, to care for his world, his human children, his Church. And the voice of God calls us all in any case to celebrate, despite all our remaining puzzles and fears, the fact that we have a God who has not left us to muddle through on our own, but who has issued in blood and fire — his own blood, his own fire — the call to follow him in his work of recreating and healing his battered and beautiful world.

Father, give us, by your Spirit, ears to hear your call, whenever and however it may come, ready wills to respond to it; and above all perseverance in obeying it to the end: through Jesus Christ, our Lord. Amen.

10

The World, the Church, and the Groaning of the Spirit

If we are God's children, we are also his heirs — heirs of God, and joint-heirs with the Messiah, provided that we suffer with him so that we may also be glorified with him. For I calculate that the sufferings of the present time do not deserve to be set alongside the glory that is to be revealed upon us; for the created order is on tiptoe with expectation, longing for the children of God to be revealed, for the created order was subjected to futility (not willingly, but through the one who subjected it) in hope — because the created order itself is to be set free from the slavery of corruption into the freedom of the glory of the children of God. For we know that the whole created order is groaning together, and is in travail together, right up to the present moment; and not only so, but also we, who have the Spirit as the first-fruits [of what is to come], we groan in ourselves as we long for our adoption, that is, the redemption of our body. For we were saved in hope; but hope that is seen is not hope, for who hopes for what is seen? But if we hope for what we do not see, we long for it with patience.

In the same way, too, the Spirit sustains and supports

us in our weakness; for we do not know how to pray as we ought, but the Spirit itself intercedes on our behalf with inarticulate groanings. And the one who searches the hearts knows the mind of the Spirit, because the Spirit is in tune with God when interceding for his people. (Romans 8.17-27)

The English are often deeply suspicious of St Paul. A senior colleague once asked me what my thesis topic had been; and when I said 'St Paul' he shook his head and said, 'A very wicked man; a very wicked man.' There is a prevalent folk-belief that Jesus founded Christianity but Paul muddled it up; or that Paul gives us a theology of legal categories while John gives us one of love. But I don't want to apologise for Paul; I want to try to let him speak for himself.

In expounding and particularly in applying St Paul, though, I do feel somewhat more apologetic on my own behalf. I am not presenting myself here as an expert from an ivory tower. My father, after many years in business, has a favourite definition of 'expert': 'x' is an unknown quantity, and a spurt is a drip under pressure. Equally, I am wary of the old definition of an Oxford college chaplain as one who dispenses sherry and agnosticism in equal proportions. Sherry is one thing, but agnosticism — well, in a certain sense I do want to offer a kind of agnosticism, because that's what Paul offers in our passage. But it's not the usual kind; it's a sort of inverted agnosticism. Most agnostics would probably say that they don't know who God might be, but they do know what he ought to be doing. As is often remarked, many people want to serve God, but only in an advisory capacity. They know what to pray *for*, but not whom to pray *to*. But what Paul says is that we don't know what to pray for; and, strangely, in that agnosticism we actually discover who God is. We are called to be the people who know whom to pray to but not, or not necessarily, what to pray *for*.

So to the text of Romans. Romans 8.17-27 comes midway between two classic 'favourite passages.' At the beginning of the chapter is the wonderful text Bach set to music in *Jesu, meine Freude:* There is now no condemnation for those who are in Christ Jesus. At the end of the chapter is the magnificent statement that neither death nor life nor anything else in all creation shall separate us from the love of God in Christ Jesus. And the road from the one to the other passes through the territory before us. There is no shortcut. This is not a backwater which can be bypassed. It is the means by which the great statements on either side escape from being mere assertions, and become grounded in theological and practical reality.

The theme of this passage is the extraordinary vocation of the people of God, within the overarching plan of God for the healing and rebirth of the entire cosmos. We are God's children, and therefore his *heirs* (v. 17a). This theme of *inheritance* resonates with the overtones of the Exodus: 'Israel is my son, my firstborn'; 'Out of Egypt I called my son.' As often in Paul, Jesus, precisely as Israel's Messiah, has taken Israel's role upon himself, enacting a new exodus and doing so on behalf of a worldwide family. And instead of the inheritance being simply one piece of sacred territory, Paul has already emphasised in chapter 4 (v. 13) that this family will inherit the world as a whole: the Promised Land in the Old Testament turns out to be a great advance metaphor for the inheritance that will come when God's plan is completely unfolded. So verse 17a: if we are God's children, we are also his heirs — heirs of God, and joint-heirs with the Messiah. The new exodus has taken place in Christ, and we are to be its beneficiaries, inheriting the *world*.

Many Christians have drawn wildly inaccurate conclusions from this belief. Some have seen the Church's task as the enforced colonisation of the world: onward Christian soldiers, fighting the good fight, letting metaphor spill over uncomfortably close to reality, and, as one recent poet said, trying to build the New Jerusalem and ending up with New York. And many other Christians, in reaction, have withdrawn from the idea of inheritance altogether: this world is not my home, I'm just a-passing through, and politics and ecology and social justice are secondary issues beside the saving of souls. Are we to rule the world, or to renounce it? Paul's answer is clear: we are to redeem it.

(i) Romans 8.17-18

This passage, then, stands over against both these misinterpretations, and points us to the genuinely Christian view of the world, and of God, and of the Church's task in between God and the world. The first move Paul makes is in 17b-18, which then get him going on his main argument. The bold statement of 17a, which we've just noted, is at once qualified: being a joint-heir with the Messiah means sharing his sufferings. Paul uses a typical sequence of Greek compounds: we are co-heirs, provided we co-suffer so that we may be co-glorified. You see, what he says about the Church is true because, and only because, the Church is 'in Christ', it is the family of the Messiah, so that what is true of him is true of them; so that they can only reach their inheritance by the path of suffering which he himself trod. Paul then explains this compressed statement in verse 18: he calculates — the word is an accounting metaphor — that the present sufferings do not add up to anything like the coming glory. And again he is open to misinterpretation. Is the Church simply exhorted to hang on stoically and wait, to grit its teeth and hope for dawn? No. Paul delves down into the Christian world-view, and explains what it means to be the people of God within God's healing plan for his whole world.

The rest of the passage consists of an argument in three stages, with the longer first stage in verses 17b-22, and the second and third in verses 23-25 and 26-27. The passage is thus rather like a threefold Russian doll; each time we open up a set of ideas, there's another one, similar but compressed, inside. Within each section, the connecting words (all the 'for's and 'because's) are vital: Paul goes on explaining things, deeper and deeper, until he reaches bedrock.

(ii) Romans 8.19-22

So to the first stage, verses 19-22, which explains the introductory verses 17-18. The created order as a whole is not evil, and to be obliterated without trace, but neither is it simply good and to be left as it stands. Follow the sequence of thought: 19, the creation is good, but incomplete; 20, good, but at present in bondage; 21, good, but awaiting liberation; 22, good, but pregnant with the future world that is to be born from its womb. Paul sets the pain and provisionality of the present creation in the context of the good purposes of the creator. So, in more detail:

Verse 19. The creation is on tiptoe with expectation: and what it's waiting for is the revelation of the children of God. Why? Because humankind was made to be the steward of creation, naming the animals and tending the garden as symbols of wise and responsible tenancy in God's world. All through Romans there runs the theme of Adam and Eve, usually implicit but sometimes explicit, as in chapter 5. And here it becomes clear that the reason for human salvation is not simply to rescue us out of the messy world, but so that through our salvation the world itself might be healed. And this will come about when humans are once again where they should be in God's intended order, under God and set in wise and loving responsibility over the world.

Paul explains this in its turn in verses 20 and 21. The creation is in bondage, and what will liberate it is the glory of God's children. As you see, I have kept the genitives at the end of verse 21 just as they are: most translators run them together ('the glorious liberty'), assuming that the creation is to share the same glory that the Church will possess. I don't think that's right. The future 'glory' of the Church is not simply that it's going to shine like an electric light bulb; there is a long Christian tradition which stresses that aspect, but I can't persuade myself that it's the most important thing here. The glory of the Church is precisely the glory which Adam lost at the Fall — that is, the wise rule over creation. Paul is here using exodus-language again, but this time in reference to the world as a whole. There is a chain of exoduses within the purposes of God: Israel coming out of Egypt, Jesus coming out of death into new life, the Church being born again in baptism, as in Romans 6, and now, amazingly, the whole cosmos. The world has been in the Egypt of futility (v. 20): this word 'futility' carries the overtones of corruption, decay, and death. The creator himself has put his creation into this strange state (v. 20), not out of anger with it but because only so, granted the rebellion of humankind, could the creation be healed. So, like the children of Israel in Egypt when Moses arrived, or like the children of Adam when Jesus appeared, the cosmos itself will one day thrill to respond to the wise rule, that is, the glory, of God's redeemed — and now redeeming — humanity. That is the vision. Instead of the worship of creation by humans, as in Romans 1, we now have creation rescued by humans. As by humans came futility, so by humans shall come freedom. The trees will clap their hands, and the valleys will laugh and sing.

And within that vision, as the climax of verses 19-22, Paul uses the great image from Genesis 3. No longer Eve, but now the whole creation, playing as it were female to God's male, is groaning together and in travail together (two more of Paul's co-words, co-groaning and co-travailing), right up to the present moment. This is the central image that Paul is now going to exploit. He cuts in behind the simplistic analyses of the world as either simply good or simply bad: he sees the world in pain, and interprets it through the great Jewish apocalyptic idea of the Messianic Woes, the birth-pangs of the new age. This great tribulation had, for Paul, been fulfilled in one way in Jesus, and was now being fulfilled in another way in the sufferings that characterised the period of the Church. The present state of the world is just this: that it is groaning in the pangs of giving birth to the new world that God desires and intends. And the result is a view of the world which leaves no room for either exploitation or idolatry. To this we shall return presently.

(iii) Romans 8.23-25

Once we have opened this first Russian doll (vv. 19-22), we find another inside. With verse 23 Paul makes the transition to his picture of the Church: 'not only so, but also we. . . .' The Church may be tempted to look on smugly and criticise the world, analyse its problems, and perhaps try to solve them, as it were from a great height. But that isn't Paul's way. For him, the Church itself is totally involved within the world, bearing in itself the same conflict, incarnating in its own life the glory and the shame, the majesty and the tragedy, that characterise creation as a whole. If the world is playing out the Eve-theme, groaning in travail as it waits for the new world to be born from its womb, so the Church is also groaning as she waits for her own full adoption. Within the exodus-metaphor, the Church has come out of Egypt but has not yet entered the promised land, the reborn cosmos, the inheritance for which she longs. Paul deliberately uses the same words for the Church as he used for the world: 'groaning' in verses 23 and 22, and 'longing' in verses 23 and 19. The female image of the Church, groaning in travail, is placed as it were within the female image of the world.

At one level the application of this should be clear. No Christian, no Church, can ever be content with things as they are. We sometimes play this down in order not to soft-pedal the Church's present task in the world. But if it is for this life only that we have hoped in Christ, we are of all people the most to be pitied; however much we work for justice and peace in our world, we cannot be true to the gospel if we do not also speak and live out of the hope that is yet to come and so as yet unseen (vv. 24-25), of an adoption, the redemption of our bodies, in the light of which we see ourselves now simply as shadows of our future selves. God has prepared for his people a fuller version of humanity than anything we can imagine, an adoption which is to be a reaffirmation of our humanness, answering completely and finally the unfulfilled longings and inexpressible yearnings of our present existence. And so, like creation, we ourselves are subjected to futility, but in patient hope (vv. 24-25). So far, so good.

But there is another level of application in verses 23-25. The parallelism between the groaning and longing of the Church (vv. 23-25) and the groaning and longing of the cosmos (vv. 19-22) means that Paul is deliberately interpreting the two in relation to each other. *The present task of the Church is not only to share the sufferings of Christ, but in doing so to share and bear the sufferings of the world* — and, indeed, to discover that those vocations are two ways of saying the same thing; so that the pain of the world, which was heaped once and for all on to the Messiah on the cross, is now strangely to be shared by those who suffer with him. The Church is not insulated from the pain of the world, but is to become for the world what Jesus was for the world, the place where its pain and grief may be focused and concentrated, and so healed. Some may feel this is a risky line of thought; faced with Romans 8, and for that matter Colossians 1.24 and 2 Corinthians 4.7-12, I am certain that it is a Pauline one. As the great contemporary American philosopher of religion, Nicholas Wolterstorff, says in the little book (*Lament for a Son,* 1987) written after the death of his son: does this mean that some of our wounds are Christ's wounds, and that some of our wounds bring healing? I think Paul's answer is Yes.

So, back to our Russian dolls. The first picture, the groaning of creation, contained clear signs that a second was hidden within it. The world waits for the Church to be redeemed. But this second picture contains, in verse 23, the clear hint that there is yet a third level, corresponding with and giving full meaning to the first two. We ourselves, who have the first-fruits of the Spirit — that is, I think, 'who have the Spirit as the down-payment of what is to come' — we ourselves groan inwardly. Once again there is a surprise. In talking about the Spirit today we are used to the note of triumph, of a supernatural dimension enabling Christians to rise above the pain and grief of the world and enter a realm of joy and peace. But that isn't Paul's picture. For him, it is precisely because of the Spirit that the Church shares the groaning

88

of the world. And how could it be otherwise, if the task laid on the Church is that she co-suffer with the Messiah? If it were not for the Spirit, such an idea might actually be blasphemous.

(iv) Romans 8.26-27

So verse 23 points us into the deep heart of the passage, verses 26-27. 'In the same way, too', Paul says in verse 26: what is true of the world and the Church is actually true also of the Spirit. *Within* the groaning of creation, and *within* the groaning of the Church, God — this strange God — is groaning also. The Spirit sustains and supports us (two English words to translate one Greek one) in our weakness. More specifically, we look at the world and long to bring to it the justice and peace, the *Shalom*, for which it is yearning. And we don't know how to do it. We don't even know how to pray, or what to pray for, as we ought. But at the very moment of this weakness, this agnosticism, we have the assurance that the Spirit is doing the praying that we cannot do. God is sharing, by his Spirit, in the groaning of creation and the groaning of the Church. But this image remains inescapably the Eve-image, the female one of giving birth. The groaning of verse 26 deliberately echoes that of verses 22 and 23. What are we to make of this? I think we should take our courage in both hands and translate verse 26b as 'we do not know how to pray as we ought, but the Spirit *herself* intercedes on our behalf with inarticulate groanings.' Prayer, at the deepest level, is here understood as God calling to God from within the created and groaning world, God calling to God from within the redeemed and groaning Church, God the Spirit, dwelling in the hearts of her people as they dwell in the midst of the broken world, and calling to God the Father, the transcendent one, and being certainly heard. The Church may be aware only of inarticulate groanings, in which it sums up not only the praises, but also the pains of creation, and brings them all before God; but the Church must also believe that this groaning is not born of itself, shouting across

89

the void to a Deist's absentee landlord, but is called forth by God himself and herself, transcendent beyond creation and also living and active deep within creation, and now, through the death and resurrection of Jesus, within the hearts of men and women. Thus, within the inner logic of the whole passage, Paul draws on the old Jewish tradition, from Genesis 1 to Proverbs and the later Wisdom writings, in which female imagery is used for the creative and healing work of God *within* creation, just as male imagery is used for the work of the transcendent God *in relation to* creation.

The Church, then, is caught up in this divine dialogue. Between the constant creative love of the Father and the deep indwelling groaning of the Spirit, the Church comes to share the pattern of the life and death and resurrection of the Son. Verse 17 stands as the rubric over the entire passage: when the world and the Church look out on the darkness and ask why they have has been abandoned, at that very moment they share the agony of the Son; so that the complaint of God's absence becomes, paradoxically, the evidence of God's presence. And the Creator, referred to in verse 27 as the heart-searcher, knows and hears; because the Spirit is interceding for God's people, literally, 'in accordance with' God, that is, in tune with God, resonating with the same loving purpose. As Cardinal Hume said on television when the Gulf War broke out, 'God was reading in my troubled heart the words and thoughts I could not myself compose.' According to Paul in these verses, the reason God was reading them is that God was putting them there in the first place.

So let us stand back from the passage as a whole and reflect on the world-view which it opens up. We live at a time of sudden and painful transitions. After centuries of implicit dualism, of a great gulf between God and the world, we are seeing the sudden rise of new pantheistic cults, of the so-called New Age movement, and even of a strident neo-paganism. And the Church must not respond to this with a reassertion of dualism, rejecting the world out of hand. Rather, we have here the ground for a fully Christian evaluation of humanness and of the world — for, one might say, a serious Christian aesthetic, enabling us to understand why the world is so achingly beautiful as well as so tragically disaster-prone, and to see both sides without either worshipping the world or rejecting it. Humans are made, Paul says, to be filled with all God's fullness. In this passage we see that the world, too, is to be flooded with God, overflowing with God, as R. S. Thomas said, as a chalice would with the sea: the Spirit who brooded over the waters of creation will bring to birth the new world, God's new creation, from the womb of the old. And that is why the world is so beautiful — not, as the materialist pagan thinks, because we can get rich out of it, nor as the New Age pagan thinks, because it is itself divine, but because it has precisely the beauty of a chalice: a vessel made not for itself but to be filled with the outpoured love of God. That is why, when we work in Christ's name for justice and peace, for beauty and truth, we do so with hope. That is why, also, we bring these things together in the Eucharist, where symbols of creation are as it were flooded in advance with the living presence of God.

And the view of God in this passage is equally striking. We in the West have assumed for too long that the word 'God' is univocal, and that we all know what it means. This passage holds out the startling picture of God as the creator *and* as the one at work to bring healing and hope within the world, *and,* in the midst of that, as the one who suffers and dies under the weight of the world's sin, and rises again as the beginning of the new creation. Paul is every bit as much a Trinitarian theologian, a theologian of the love of God, as is John. And the world still waits to hear about this God.

I want, in conclusion, to apply this briefly where it may matter most. Most Christians for most of the time have people on their hearts and minds, people in pain who have asked our prayers. If you're like me, half the time you won't know what to pray for. But in that inarticulate state there is a longing, a groaning, a resonating with their pain, which tells us that we are becoming on their behalf the place of prayer, of the Spirit's prayer, the prayer too deep for words. Without that possibility and reality I sometimes wonder how one could engage in pastoral work at all.

More particularly, there are crises in the world about which we simply don't know what to pray for. I suspect, actually, that crises merely reveal our normal state. We fool ourselves into thinking that we've worked out the answers, that we've got the world taped; and then a war, or a sudden tragedy, shakes us out of that complacency, and into the recognition that we need prayer beyond our own prayer. How can this happen?

In my college chapel in Oxford, during the Gulf War, the students made a small display on the floor beside the altar — a pile of sand with some poppies, and a single candle in the middle. Those of us who went in there every day didn't know how to pray, what to pray for. But we knelt there, in front of the sand and the poppies, and looked up at the cross on the great stained-glass window above, and simply tried, without words and often with puzzlement and grief, to put the two of them together: to let the God revealed in Jesus embrace and hold within himself the Gulf and all that it was and meant. And that, I think, isn't a step down from Christian clarity to sub-Christian puzzlement. I think it may be a step up from (if you like) O-level prayer to A-level prayer. Of course there are many things we can and must still pray for in words. But when words fail us, God does not. And in the agony of our hearts, in the unanswered questions, in the pain as we identify with the peoples of the Middle East, not to mention the pain of our own people and of others around the world — in all this we begin to resonate with the pain of the world, and to know in faith that we are also resonating with the pain of God. And so we become the place and the means of joining together God and the world — the dying love of Jesus and the pile of sand and poppies — the redeeming power of cross, resurrection, and Spirit and the brokenness of the whole human race: so that the two sides of reality are held together within our own humanness, our puzzlement, our own brokenness, hopes, and fears. If that's not prayer, I don't know what is:

And so the yearning strong
With which the soul will long

Shall far outpass the power of human telling.
For none can guess its grace
Till he become the place
Wherein the Holy Spirit makes her dwelling —

and not only makes her dwelling, but utters her groaning, to bring to birth the new people who will be flooded with God, to bring to birth the new world that will be flooded with God, until the earth shall be filled with the glory of God as the waters cover the sea.

And the task of the Church, not least its leaders and representatives in Synods and elsewhere, is to live through this process of prayer, of longing and groaning, and then to seek to create and facilitate structures through which the Church will be able more effectively to be the people of *this* God for *this* world. The Church is awfully good at masking its puzzlement, by passing thundering resolutions or clinging to impossibly sub-Christian formulations, so as not to hear its own groanings, so as to screen out the pain of its own paradoxical existence; and so we fail to resonate with the pain of the world — and so fail to become the dwelling place, and groaning place, of God. It is as if Jesus, coming over the top of the Mount of Olives, had smiled sardonically at Jerusalem's coming fate, instead of nearly choking with tears. Or again we may avoid this theme by so eagerly affirming the world as it stands that we ignore its brokenness and absolutize its present temporary state, as though the groaning were simply the rumbling of a full belly. Either way, the Church is too ready to avoid the peculiar vocation that is here held out. Synods and committees — and for that matter biblical scholars — can be great *instruments of* the work of the Spirit; they cannot be *substitutes for* it. And the way to become such instruments is through the serious prayer which is called forth *by* the Spirit, enacted in the Eucharist (which is the focus of so much that I have said in this chapter) and which overflows into theology, politics, work in society, art, medicine, healing at every level. It is in this process, this rhythm of prayer and work, that we are caught up into the life and love of the triune God, and with that are given what we all need at the present time, and that is hope:

And for all this nature is never spent;
There lives the dearest freshness deep down things;
And though the last lights off the black West went
Oh, morning, at the brown brink Eastward springs —
Because the Holy Ghost over the bent
World broods with warm breast and with Ah! bright wings.
(Gerard Manley Hopkins, God's Grandeur)

Father, give us your own Spirit, that we may be able to hear the groaning of your wounded world; that we may take our part in the groaning of the church as we await our full adoption; and that we may ourselves resonate with the agony and the hope which is your own: through Jesus Christ our Lord. Amen.

11

Eucharist and the Presence of Christ

As Jesus came near and saw Jerusalem, he wept over it, saying, 'If you, even you, had only recognized on this day the things that make for peace! But now they are hidden from your eyes. Indeed, the days will come upon you, when your enemies will set up ramparts around you and surround you, and hem you in on every side. They will crush you to the ground, you and your children within you, and they will not leave within you one stone upon another; because you did not recognize the time of your visitation from God.'

Then he entered the temple and began to drive out those who were selling things there; and he said, 'It is written, "My house shall be a house of prayer"; but you have made it a den of brigands.' (Luke 19.41-46 NRSV)

I have spoken so far of the dying love of Christ, and of the challenge of putting it into operation in the world. I have mentioned, fairly briefly, the Church's responsibility to apply the unique truth of Calvary to the world at large. But just as many

Christians still fight shy of embracing their responsibility in society, so many — often, alas, the same ones — still retreat from embracing their resources in the sacraments. It seems to me that these two do indeed go together, and in what follows I want to try to integrate them, to put together what I have said about the purposes of God for his world with a way of understanding the Eucharist in particular.

'You did not recognize the time of your visitation from God.' Or, in another version, 'You did not recognize God's moment when it came,' when your God came incognito into your midst. That is Jesus' great indictment of his Jewish contemporaries. They were so busy with their own concerns, in particular their questions of national security or of national purity, that when at long last God came to fulfil his promises they were looking the wrong way. As a result, it was not only God and his visitation of which they were ignorant: it was also their own fate. 'If only you had known — on this day — even you — the things which make for peace: but now they are hidden from your eyes.' That sentence in Greek is jerky and disjointed. It is wrung out of Jesus in great sobs and tears. Jerusalem is the joy of the whole earth, and it has turned its joy into pride, its beauty into ashes. The only word it can hear now is the word of judgment: you have made God's house a brigand's den. God is visiting his people, and Israel doesn't know it.

The hidden presence of God in the midst of his people is a major theme in St Luke's Gospel. After an earlier healing miracle, the crowds say, 'A great prophet has risen up among us,' and 'God has visited his people.' And that theme, of God dwelling with his people, automatically reminds a Jew of the temple. The temple was first and foremost the place where God lived. The thing which marked out the Jews from all other nations was that they believed that the creator of the earth was their God, and lived in their midst. The idea of a god dwelling in a temple was not of course unique to Judaism: in some ways, it seems a very pagan idea. Every pagan temple had a shrine with an image of the god who lived there, and the image actually made the god present. Judaism, though, was different. It had no image. Or rather, it had no carved or chiselled inanimate image, because its God was not like that. He was the creator of the world, not just one god among many, and he already had an image, which could not be bettered however hard a sculptor might try: a living, breathing image called humankind, and now Israel herself, called as she was to be his true humanity, his true image, reflecting him in his world, being his presence in his world.

And Jesus comes to fulfil that hope and that destiny. Israel's God was not remote or detached, nor was he simply a nature god or a tribal god. He was the creator of the world, and at the same time lived in and with and amongst his people. That was what the temple was all about; and it was why the temple was the place of sacrifice, because there the holy God met with sinful people and, miracle upon miracle, instead of burning them up forgave them and restored them as members of his people.

And now Jesus comes and declares God's judgment on the temple itself. God's house has become a brigand's den; Israel has used the temple as a talisman, a mascot, a good-luck charm; but God is not mocked. He will come to her; he will come, as he has promised; but when he comes, judgment will begin at the household of God. To a nation sunk in its own conviction that it is right, God will come as a fire, as a hammer that breaks rock in pieces, as a prophet who drives out the traders with a whip and a word of Scripture. God's visitation of Israel is a secret visitation of judgment.

But it is also a secret visitation of mercy. Again, as we saw earlier, Jesus' healing miracles, and his regular and habitual table fellowship with sinners, were signs that what the temple stood for within Israel was now being fulfilled at a deeper level. Where Jesus is, God is present with his people, reconstituting them, restoring them, healing them, forgiving their sins. Here God's presence in Jesus is still secret, but this time because the truth is so enormous that it cannot be fully grasped: that God does not ultimately dwell in bricks and mortar, but in and as a human being, his true Image, his own Son. Jesus is the true temple, that

for which the beautiful temple in Jerusalem was only the proto-
type: so that where he is, God is living in the midst of his people,
in solemn judgment and in astonishing mercy. Jesus is, if you
like, the mode of God's presence with his people (remembering
that 'mode' is here simply a musical metaphor, not a subtle bit
of philosophising).

But how does God then become present in his world today?
We who live after the ascension of Jesus, and before his final
return, have to face the question: how can what happened two
thousand or so years ago be of continuing significance for the
world? We may believe *that* it is so, but we are hard pressed to
explain *how* it is so, especially when asked by a sceptic or cynic.
And the Church has traditionally given two sorts of answers. The
first is to try to show that the presence of God in Christ has been
continued, transmitted, throughout subsequent history, in and
through the Church and the sacraments. The second is to suggest
that God, being essentially outside time and space, can relate to
all time and space equally, by his Spirit, so that we creatures of
time can be touched, as it were at a tangent, by God who meets
us from outside time.

Let us reflect for a moment on those two views. The first,
which sees God at work within history, takes with complete
seriousness the fact that in Jesus (and actually in the creation of
the world and in the history of Israel) God has committed himself
to working *within* the space-time process. This, as should by now
be clear, I regard as utterly biblical and utterly nonnegotiable.
The second — seeing God breaking into history from outside —
takes completely seriously the fact that God is not simply part of
the space-time process, that we cannot simply imprison him
within either the world of nature or the machinery of the Church's
life. This too I regard as utterly biblical and utterly nonnegotiable.
The trouble is, of course, that the two views are normally con-
ceived as irreconcilable, not just in tension but in flagrant mutual
contradiction. And the further trouble, indeed the further tragedy,
is that these battles are brought to a head at the point where the
Church should be united, that is, the Eucharist. For the one view

has suggested, as part of its whole theology of God at work within the historical process, that in the bread and the wine Jesus becomes really and in a sense physically present, and the other has suggested that in the Lord's Supper Jesus relates to his people in a purely spiritual way, with the bread and the wine serving merely as a sign or a reminder of a fact that is essentially nonphysical. And so, where we should have joy and excitement at our celebration of Jesus' fellowship meal, we have controversy and tragedy. The Eucharist, and the question of Jesus' presence at it, has become a problem instead of a privilege.

The historical setting of this problem is of some relevance, and we must look at it briefly. For our purposes the story starts in the mediaeval definitions of Christ's presence in the Eucharist. The mediaeval Church believed implicitly that Jesus was present with his people when they met together to worship, and especially when they met to celebrate the Eucharist. And Jesus had said, 'This is my body.' How could they understand this strange truth? They were faced with the task of articulating how it was that Jesus met his faithful people in this meal, and came up with a solution dependent on a particular metaphysical system. Think of a rose. This rose happens to have certain petal formations, a particular smell, prickles of a certain shape and distribution. These are, in a sense, accidental. They might have been different without the rose's ceasing to be what it is. They are therefore to be called the 'accidents' of the rose, while the 'substance' of the rose is a mysterious entity, what we might call its roseness, which cannot be expressed in, or reduced to terms of, its mere accidents, its particular molecules.

Now take this scheme and apply it to bread, the bread of the Eucharist. When Jesus celebrated the Last Supper, he said, 'This is my body', and then said, 'Do this in remembrance of me.' How do we do justice to these words without at the same time talking nonsense? The distinction of substance and accidents seemed to offer an answer. The *substance* of Christ's body — not of course the accidents, his actual skin or actual flesh, but what we might call his Christness — is mysteriously transferred to the

bread. It replaces, not the accidents of the bread — its own particular actual molecules — but its substance, its breadness, the
mysterious and invisible bread-in-itself which lies 'behind' or as
it were 'underneath' the mere accidents. And so there was born
the developed theology of transubstantiation. It had nothing
whatever to do with a crude idea of Jesus' literal flesh replacing
the literal molecules of the bread. It was a way of asserting, despite
the sense-evidence to the contrary — which of course could only
detect or 'pick up' the 'accidents' — that Jesus was really present,
as he himself had apparently said, in the bread and the wine. The
alternative would have been, for the mediaeval theologian, to have
said that Jesus was really absent, that he was simply not present
at all: and that was of course unthinkable. To this extent, as some
Roman Catholic theologians are now saying, the doctrine of transubstantiation was a mediaeval answer to a mediaeval question.
If you insist on asking the question in those terms, that is the
right answer. Better transubstantiation than an absent Jesus.

But do we have to ask that question and use that metaphysic?
That was the question posed most sharply by the Reformers. They
were faced, as far as they could see, with a system that had gone
sour. The great scheme of God at work in history, in the Church,
the priesthood and the Mass, had produced, as they saw it,
superstition, corruption, and exploitation. And they insisted instead, in their various ways, that transubstantiation was wrong.
They quarrelled among themselves over this. Luther stayed with
the apparent literal sense of Christ's words of institution, but
suggested what he called 'consubstantiation' — the substance of
the bread is still there, and Christ's substance is now joined to it.
Zwingli denied this, and saw the bread as a 'bare sign', pointing
beyond itself, enabling the worshipper to recall Christ to mind,
and so — since he is present wherever two or three gather in his
name — to make him 'spiritually' present. Calvin, easily the most
creative of the three in this and in many other things, suggested
that the 'real presence' was not Christ's presence here on an altar
or table, but the presence of the worshippers, by the action of
God's Holy Spirit, in heaven itself. This view is close to that of

the Eastern Orthodox Church. 'Lift up your hearts', we say: we are taken up, in the Spirit, to the place where Christ really is present, and there we really do feed on him. The English Reformers were more cautious again: at his trial Archbishop Cranmer insisted *both* that the bread remains bread *and* that a real feeding takes place, and one of the noblest elements of that sorry business was the way in which he was prepared to die at the stake for the combination of two beliefs which he seems never to have reconciled. And so the Church in the West has been bequeathed, this last four hundred years, a legacy of suspicion and mistrust, of misunderstanding and confusion, so that instead of the Eucharist being a glad united feast it has often been the centre of division.

In terms of spiritual warfare, this situation is disastrous. That which is most powerful and important is the thing most readily attacked and put out of action. Paul says, 'As often as you break this bread and drink this cup, you show forth the Lord's death until he comes.' Celebrating this meal announces to the world that the crucified Jesus is Lord! What could be more powerful than that, to confront the powers of this age with the judgment and mercy of God in Christ? Small wonder that attention has been diverted from this central assault on the powers that oppose the gospel. The would-be attackers have instead been fighting each other over how precisely their main battering ram 'works'. Or, which is just as bad, they have simply stopped using the weapon altogether, for fear of squabbles. A good example of this occurred in 1989, when a group of Christians, claiming to be following the Bible to the last letter, held a large and well-publicised meeting in Manila to discuss the evangelisation of the world. The title of the meeting was 'Proclaim Christ Until He Comes'. But nowhere in their deliberations or in the official report of the meeting was there any suggestion of taking seriously the biblical context of that quotation. According to Paul in 1 Corinthians 11.26, Christ is proclaimed to the world when the Church performs the actions of breaking bread and pouring out wine in his name. Mission is more than just words.

101

I believe we have in our generation a chance to put this right. Rome wasn't built in a day — perhaps an unhappy metaphor in this context — but there has been building going on quietly for some while now, and we are within sight of new things which previous generations have longed and prayed for. We have started to recognise that underneath the hardened old battle positions with which the two (Western) factions of Christ's army have fought each other there are world-views which themselves need challenging, and that it has been the attempt to express God's truth — Christ's truth — within the framework of these world-views that has caused us to fight each other instead of celebrating with each other the victory of Christ over the powers of evil. Theologians in various camps have started to explore different ways of asserting what needs to be asserted without denying what must not be denied, and have been finding some common ground. The Anglican–Roman Catholic discussions have made considerable progress, despite the somewhat frosty reception they have been given both by the Vatican and by the more suspicious of Protestant Anglicans. New words have been cautiously tried out, among them 'transignification', the idea that the bread changes not its substance but its meaning, not as a piece of sympathetic magic but as part of the whole action of the Eucharist, which creates its own new context of meaning.

But I think we can go further than this. As usual, though, we can only go forward by going back. We must go back, for a start, to the Bible. In the Old Testament the prophets often perform strange symbolic actions which somehow actually accomplish that of which they speak. Ezekiel takes a brick and says, 'This is Jerusalem.' And what he does to the brick *happens*, in historical reality, to Jerusalem. Jesus, in the same way, takes bread and says, 'This is my body', and breaks it; and then goes out to die. And Paul, warning the early Christians of the dangers of coming casually and flippantly to this meal, speaks of those who eat and drink judgment upon themselves because they do not 'discern the body.' They, like Jerusalem on the first Palm Sunday, fail to recognise the time of divine visitation.

102

But, behind all such language and our understanding of it, what are we talking about when we are talking about bread and wine, God and man, Christ and our poor selves? We are talking about God and the world; and it is scarcely surprising if at this point our language should let us down, if our words themselves should become temples from which the presence of God seems mysteriously to have vanished, temples which have even become dens of brigands, battlegrounds of warring factions, more anxious to condemn than to adore, to be doctrinally sound than to love and be loved. What can we say, we whose very words about the presence of God stand under the judgment of the presence of God, whose language of divine visitation is itself judged by divine visitation?

To look for appropriate words we must, I believe, make a long journey: a journey to the end of time. Then, we are told by the prophet, the earth shall be filled with the knowledge of the glory of the Lord, as the waters cover the sea. Now that's an odd phrase. How do the waters cover the sea? They *are* the sea. And how then will the glory of the Lord fill the earth? It will *be* the earth. What am I saying? That God made a world that was other than himself in order to flood it with himself; that the glory we see in a sunset or in a child's eyes is the glory of anticipation; not that the world is God but that it is made for God, and already reflects in its transient glory, and aches for in its glorious transience, that glorious filling for which it was made. What am I saying? That God in Christ and by his Spirit has decisively begun the last stage towards that glorious filling, that irradiating of the world with himself. He has taken human clay and clothed himself with it, or rather has *become* it, in the incarnation, dwelling incognito among his people in judgment and mercy. He has, further, taken more human clay and, by his Spirit, has clothed himself with it, has *become* it, again and again, as men, women, and children are transformed by his secret judging and healing presence in their lives.

And, of course, when human beings are remade in God's image, they begin to be set once more in authority over the world.

Where Jesus was, storms were stilled, lepers were healed, loaves and fishes were multiplied; creation leapt into new life at the touch of God incarnate, God incognito. We see in the life and ministry of Jesus a foretaste of the splendour that will one day fill the earth as the waters cover the sea.

And in the Eucharist we therefore not only look *back* to Jesus, we look *on* to Jesus. As we strain our eyes forward we see, we glimpse, his plan for the whole created order. The earth shall be filled with the glory of God as the waters cover the sea — as the human being Jesus was filled with the glory of God, the glory that was revealed supremely on the cross, because it is the glory of love. The whole earth is to resound with the glory of God as Jesus did, answering to its creator as he answered to his Father. And how is it to do that? How can bread redound to the glory of God? How can wine sing his praises? By becoming charged afresh with the grandeur of God, taken up into his purposes and becoming the true food of human beings. And, since the food we most deeply need is the judging and healing presence of God himself, that his death may be our death and his life our life, this food is none other than Christ himself, God incarnate, God incognito. So it is that, within the whole action of the Eucharist, Christ meets us in bread and wine; meets us not just as a figure of the past but also as the figure to whom belongs the future: God, present with his people in judgment and mercy, in broken bread and poured out wine. This is what the universe was made for, that it might be the vehicle of God's glory. And as we take our place, humbly and obediently, worshipping God the Father, in the person of his Son and the power of his Spirit, the world becomes for a moment, in the symbols of bread and wine, what in God's good time it will be for ever: the true vehicle of the true Christ.

This is not idolatry, as though we were to worship bread and wine or indulge in some quasi-Christian form of paganism (as Protestantism has always suspected of Catholics). Nor is it dualism or rationalism, as though we were to hold God and the world firmly apart (as Catholics have always suspected of Protestants).

It is *both* the continuation of an unbroken line of history, within which God is continually at work, *and* the intersection of eternity and time. If we insist on pressing our mediaeval, or our rationalist, world-views and questions — is Jesus physically present or is he physically absent? — the truth will for ever elude us. We need a new metaphysic, a new ontology, to do justice to the truth, of God and the world, which is here encapsulated.

And in the Eucharist we are given exactly that. Here is the new divine visitation which we are bidden to recognize as it comes. The church is in danger of being too busy with its own concerns — not least its debates about whether our God *ought* to do such a thing, and, if so, how such a thing might best be fitted into the little boxes of our own theological understanding. We may, like the Jews of Jesus' day, be looking the wrong way, and so miss the glory and terror of the moment. Here is the presence of God, in Christ, by the Spirit. It is the presence of Jesus of Nazareth, the crucified and risen one, in the midst of his people as the new temple, the place where the God of love and grace is to be met in love and gratitude. It is the presence of the one who judges and remakes us, who judges (in particular) our divisions and calls us (in particular) to love one another in him. It is the presence of the one to whom the angels ceaselessly sing Alleluia. It is the living presence of the living God. It is the loving presence of the loving God.

Father, as we thank you for the promise that you will make all things new, we thank you especially for the anticipation of this renewal which we enjoy as we share the banquet of your Son. Grant us understanding of this mystery, but above all the knowledge of your presence and love which passes understanding: through Jesus Christ our Lord. Amen.

12

The Fire, the Rose, and the Wounded Surgeon

Was our society, which had always been so assured of its superiority and rectitude, so confident of its unexamined premisses, — was our society assembled round anything more permanent than a congeries of banks, insurance companies and industries, and had it any beliefs more essential than a belief in compound interest and the maintenance of dividends? (T. S. Eliot, *The Idea of a Christian Society*)

That is the question which T. S. Eliot posed as the starting point, and excuse, for the book he wrote just before the outbreak of the Second World War. Faced as he was with Europe in 1939, with new paganism to the left and right, he discovered that the government of England had nothing to offer with which to oppose or even meet the challenge. He was not, as he said, criticising the government, but rather questioning the validity of a whole civilisation. It seemed to me in 1989, on the fiftieth anniversary of his lectures, that many of his predictions had been fulfilled; and nothing in the last two years has made me alter my opinion. And what I want to do here is to reflect on the question as Eliot posed it, using words from his poetry as well as his prose. I do so in the belief that there is something to be said for getting one's hands dirty with actual problems, instead of sitting around waiting passively for a perfect solution to be parachuted down from heaven. If all (or even some) of what I have said so far in this book is true, that isn't the way in which the creator works.

The first thing to be done, in fact, is to question the idea of the perfect solution itself. I suspect that sometimes, not least in thinking of a book with a title like *The Idea of a Christian Society,* we have the picture in our minds that somewhere, if only we could find it, there is a blueprint of what the ideal Christian society might look like. Our task would then be to discover the blueprint and to attempt to put it into operation, whether by persuasion or coercion. And of course as soon as we think of that, our hearts fail us. We doubt the possibility of persuading our contemporaries to follow the Christian way, and we recognise that to coerce them (which, I suppose, was what our own Civil War was all about) seems to us now to cut off the branch on which we claim to be sitting, to try to enforce the sword of the gospel with the gospel of the sword.

> And what shall we say of the future? Is one church
>   all we can build?
> Or shall the Visible Church go on to conquer the World?
> (Choruses from The Rock X)

This dilemma is, I think, more of our making than of Eliot's. He clearly says (p. 67) that for him 'Idea' doesn't mean a static thing, a generalised blueprint, but rather that conception of a thing 'which is given by the knowledge of its ultimate aim'. In other words, we must discern the direction and ultimate destination in which God wants us to move: the Christian society will not necessarily be the one which has arrived at its destination, but the one which is on the way, which is in existence as a pilgrim, en route from the present age to that which is to come.

And here we surely need the vision supplied in the book of Revelation:

> I saw a new heaven and a new earth; for the first heaven and the first earth had passed away, and the sea was no more. And I saw the holy city, new Jerusalem, coming down out of heaven from God, prepared as a bride adorned for her husband; and I heard a loud voice from the throne, saying, 'Behold, the dwelling of God is with men. He will dwell with them, and they shall be his people, and God himself will be with them; he will wipe away every tear from their eyes. . . .' And he who sat upon the throne said, 'Behold, I make all things new.' (Revelation 21.1-5 RSV)

The idea of a Christian society cannot be an idea of a perfect state of affairs that could in principle be instituted tomorrow, or next year, by the adjustment of a few nuts and bolts or even by a major upheaval or revolution, and which would then, with a sigh of relief, just go on being a Christian society for ever and ever, Amen. If we are talking Christian sense about it, we must mean two things: first, the vision of the new heaven and the new earth which God himself will inaugurate, for which we can long and pray but which we ourselves can never build by ourselves; and, second, the idea of a society which is not just longing and praying but which is seeking to be obedient to that vision, as best it can, in a present time which is inherently unlike that future state. The idea of a Christian society must therefore always be paradoxical, because we are called to put into provisional effect something which can never in the present age reach its consummation. '"Our citizenship is in heaven"; yes, but that is the model and type for your citizenship upon earth.'

This first point — the provisionality of all our attempts to realise a Christian society here and now — is further filled out by my second point: that the main characteristic of this paradoxical present stage is to be, not the imposition of an ideal from above, but the continuous healing of the disease from below. As

Eliot grew older, he became more and more aware of the fact of sin and evil, not as incidental and regrettable features of society but as deeply engrained within the nature of humankind. He held before himself and his readers a vision of England, an England with a great and noble past and a squalid and traitorous present:

> The desert is not remote in southern tropics,
> The desert is not only around the corner,
> The desert is squeezed in the tube-train next to you,
> The desert is in the heart of your brother.
>
> (Choruses from *The Rock* I)

And what Eliot saw in the unemployment of the 1930s is repeated in the different but related human sufferings of our own day. At the heart of it there is, soaked into so much modern consciousness that we almost take it for granted, a sense of life that is purposeless, rootless, and meaningless:

> A thousand policemen directing the traffic
> Cannot tell you why you come or where you go.
>
> (Choruses from *The Rock* III)

Thus, within the vision of a Christian society — and not merely as a tool to bring it about — Eliot uses in one of his greatest poems the image of the wounded surgeon: the surgeon who operates on the sick person but who is himself bleeding, wounded, suffering. This is the Christ-image, stark and shocking as the crucifixion would be stark and shocking if we had not become used to it.

And this strange work of Jesus is in some sense, as we have been thinking, continued by the Church. The Church does not have the blueprint for Christian society in its pocket, to hand down to the world with a patronising smile. It has a different kind of print to offer, the print of the nails in its hands and feet, the marks of the wounds which are the only qualification for admission to the guild of surgeons. The Church does not wave a magic wand, to banish all ills from society at a stroke. It holds up the cross, the cross of Jesus, its own cross, its mark of identity, an identity which is by its very nature the opposite of the triumphalist vision in which the Church has the answers and the world simply needs to listen, admit its folly, and change its ways. The answer that the Church does have is the answer God himself made on Calvary to the strident anger of the world: the silent answer of suffering love.

But what does this mean in practice? How can the Church make this answer to the pains of the world, and so become the sign and even the means of a Christian society in the form appropriate to it in this age? It would, perhaps, be easy to propound some grand theory which would fit South Africa, or perhaps North America, or some other place where one does not happen to live oneself, and whose pains and prospects are not one's own. Eliot was more realistic. Looking round at the neo-paganism of Germany and Russia, he turned his attention, in his prose and his poetry, to England. He inquired what had gone wrong: he saw the Church implicated continually in that wrong: and he wrestled with the question of how things might be put right. And, three years after writing *The Idea of a Christian Society,* he completed in 1942 the fourth of his *Four Quartets,* named after that strange and beautiful place of community and prayer, Little Gidding. Here he wrestles once more with the question of what England is, of where she has come from and where she must go, and of how, in the strange working of God, England could again become a place where God is honoured. The quiet community and its inner life of prayer becomes a sign of what can and must be:

> There are other places
> Which are also the world's end, some at the sea jaws,
> Or over a dark lake, in a desert or a city —
> But this is the nearest, in place and time,
> Now and in England.

And England, seen under the image of the rose, the rose which once was and now is simply ash on an old man's sleeve, this

111

England can again become the place where the fire of God's love and grace once more catches hold. Here is the paradoxical beginning of the rebirth of the Christian society:

> If you came this way,
> Taking any route, starting from anywhere,
> At any time or at any season,
> It would always be the same: you would have to put off
> Sense and notion . . .
> Here, the intersection of the timeless moment
> Is England and nowhere. Never and always.

To live without the fire of God's refining and restoring is to court bitterness and defeat, to have all our dreams and even all our virtues weighed in the balance and found wanting. It is only in a fresh anointing of the Holy Spirit that human society can escape the vicious circle of its own follies:

> The only hope, or else despair
> Lies in the choice of pyre or pyre —
> To be redeemed from fire by fire.

And the poem ends in the eventual union of the fire and the rose, of the fire of God's purifying and healing love and the rose which is the true society God has willed for this country. 'Little Gidding' and *The Idea of a Christian Society* need, I think, to be read in the light of one another.

But it's all very well to talk grandly about 'England.' We don't think quite like that now: in our cynicism we have abandoned even nationalism, and would sell England cheerfully if we thought we would gain a better rate of interest thereby. And even if we do yearn for God to send his refining and healing fire on this nation, this could remain simply at the level of dreams and prayers, of romantic idealism, or of a detached pietism that would bring 'spiritual' nourishment for some at the cost of society's still going on its pagan way. What I want to suggest is that *we* have the chance — and, more, the vocation — to explore and discover what it might mean to be a Christian society, in the various communities in which we find ourselves. I write with the image of a college community in mind — a community of very different individuals, with different social and racial backgrounds, different ages, different needs, problems, hopes, and fears. What I have to say could quite easily be transposed into other, smaller settings, which reflect, in their own little but quite significant ways, the follies, and the vocations, of society at large.

Consider for a moment the large, and then the small, picture. England, particularly when you come back to it from being away for some years, is a place of great insecurity. We had a perpetual financial crisis for long enough under the Labour party; we have now had perpetual political and social tension under the Tories. We are an increasingly divided nation, with mutual jealousies and suspicions, fears and hostilities. Violence is planned in cold blood and put into operation against people to whom no personal malice is borne, save for the fact that their football scarf is the wrong colour. We band together into groups, the more powerful for their being unofficial: classes, accents, regional loyalties, types of employment. Those who are most consumed by these things become politicians, and shout at each other across the House of Commons. And what does the Church do? Does it renounce this factionalism? Does it declare that there is neither Jew nor Greek, slave nor free, male nor female? Does it, day by day, engage in proclamation and symbolic actions which show that this way of life is a way of death? Does it call down the refining fire of God on this faded and jaded rose of England? No. It prefers to play its own version of the same game. The Church faces its own insecurity factors — the rise of Enlightenment thought and modern science, growing scepticism, and increasing awareness of the tremendous scale of the actual human plight (as opposed to the little sins of isolated individuals). And so the Church retreats into its own shelters, its own cliques and ghettos. The Church declares, in actual proclamation and effective symbol, that it is more important to be low-church or high-church than to be Christian

113

rather than non-Christian; that it is more important to be Anglican, or Roman Catholic, or Methodist, or Brethren, than to speak
for Jesus and his lordship to a world aching for the touch of the
wounded surgeon; that it is more important to keep the fire in
the correct fireplace than to let it near the Rose that so desperately
needs it.

And how, in any given microcosm of society, do we mirror
the wider society in which we find ourselves? University life
(taking my own example) may look glittering from the outside,
but it's rather different from close up. We too are insecure. Academic life consists of the daily and weekly facing of insecurity
and the attempt to get around it, to understand the apparently
incomprehensible, to learn the apparently unlearnable, in time
for the next class, the next essay, the looming exam or (from the
teachers' point of view) the next lecture, the overdue book, the
chance of promotion. And life in general consists in a similar daily
and weekly facing of insecurity: my anxious need to be befriended
by those I admire, to have my skills applauded by my peers, to
be loved by the one I secretly love. And how do we cope with
these and other insecurities? We take the route of retreat: we
withdraw into ourselves, let the world go hang, do our own thing;
and we shrink. Or we huddle together for warmth with those
who, because they are so like us, do not threaten us in the way
the rest of the folk do; and we form cliques, which (whether we
desire it or not) exclude, and, in excluding, wound, those who
have not such easy access to illusory warmth. To diagnose is not
to condemn; but it is necessary to see things clearly if healing is
to follow.

And what does the Church in a community say to those
around it who are in pain, due to their insecurity and their feelings
— whether justifiable or not — of rejection? Does the Christian
community take thought to understand the pain of those around,
and to share it, feeling the wound in itself and so able to heal the
wounds of those around? Sometimes there are signs of exactly
that, and we may rejoice that the Church in our own generation
is beginning to respond to this call. But we also see, and feel, and

taste in the air from time to time, the threat of the Church falling victim to the same insecurities: the huddling together for warmth with those who are intrinsically like-minded or from the same background; the perpetuation of old battles long outdated, the revival of antagonisms from another generation. But if it is warmth we want, we are bidden to find it not in the hot-water bottles of mere like-mindedness, but in the fire of a love which refines and changes us as we learn to accept one another in Christ:

> Love is the unfamiliar Name
> Behind the hands that wove
> The intolerable shirt of flame
> Which human power cannot remove.
> We only live, only suspire
> Consumed by either fire or fire.

And to any mood of factionalism — against which we must always be on our guard — Eliot again has the right word:

> We cannot revive old factions
> We cannot restore old policies
> Or follow an antique drum.
> These men, and those who opposed them
> And those whom they opposed
> Accept the constitution of silence
> And are folded in a single party . . .
> And all shall be well and
> All manner of thing shall be well
> By the purification of the motive
> In the ground of our beseeching.

What then is the vision we must and may have for a Christian society within the community of which we are aware? Not, as Eliot rightly says, for the instant conversion of every member of a community to explicit Christian belief. We must, of course, always work and pray for the presentation of the

115

gospel to all our neighbours, but we can and must do more than this, not less. We must be, not as an *extension* of our basic discipleship but as its proper and natural *expression,* the wounded community that brings healing to the society around us; the community that feels the pain of the world, the depression and the worry and the anger and the exclusion and the hopelessness that are the daily lot of those around; and thus the community that, being itself healed by the wounded healer himself, can pass on that healing to its neighbours. By such means communities are changed, whether or not their members explicitly adopt Christianity. By such people God is honoured as his human creatures become more fully themselves, and as in a mystery the final triumph of God is anticipated: 'The dwelling of God is with men. He will dwell with them, and they shall be his people, and God himself will be with them; he will wipe away every tear from their eyes.' By this light shall the nations walk: when Jerusalem is glorified, the nations will see it and know that God is here. The Idea of a Christian Society is a vision, *partly* realised but also partly *realised,* in which the people of God enact the love of God, in and through their own wounds and healing, for the benefit and thus the transformation of the society around them. It is a vision of a Christian community, and hence of a Church, a country and a world, purified and transformed by the fire of God's wounded love:

> So, while the fight fails
> On a winter's afternoon, in a secluded chapel
> History is now and England.

We must, then, recognise with Eliot that the vision of the new Jerusalem is not a blueprint that we have in our briefcases to present to Parliament. Nor is it simply a pietist's charter; nor yet something that leaves us 'Christians at our devotions and merely secular reformers all the rest of the week' (*The Idea of a Christian Society,* p. 99). We taste our vocation in Eucharist, we feel the pain of the shirt of fire around us day by day, and we catch on the edge of the wind, in poem and symbol, that which ever eludes our knowledge and yet which we know most deeply:

> We shall not cease from exploration
> And the end of all our exploring
> Will be to arrive where we started
> And know the place for the first time.
> Through the unknown, remembered gate
> When the last of earth left to discover
> Is that which was the beginning;
> At the source of the longest river
> The voice of the hidden waterfall
> And the children in the apple-tree
> Not known, because not looked for
> But heard, half-heard, in the stillness
> Between two waves of the sea.
> Quick now, here, now, always
> A condition of complete simplicity
> (Costing not less than everything)
> And all shall be well and
> All manner of thing shall be well
> When the tongues of flame are in-folded
> Into the crowned knot of fire
> And the fire and the rose are one.

Father, give to us and all your people such a vision of your love, and such an understanding of the needs of our society, that we may be the means of bringing the two together, to the glory of your name and the healing of your world: through the fire of your Spirit and in the name of Jesus Christ our Lord. Amen.

13

That the World May be Healed

My God, my God, why have you forsaken me?
Why are you so far from helping me, from the words
    of my groaning?
O my God, I cry by day, but you do not answer;
    and by night, but find no rest.
Yet you are holy, enthroned on the praises of Israel.
In you our ancestors trusted; they trusted,
    and you delivered them.
To you they cried, and were saved; in you they trusted,
    and were not put to shame.
But I am a worm, and not human; scorned by others,
    and despised by the people.
All who see me mock at me; they make mouths at me,
    they shake their heads;
'Commit your cause to the Lord, let him deliver —
    let him rescue the one in whom he delights! . . .

I will tell of your name to my brothers and sisters;
    in the midst of the congregation I will praise you:
You who fear the Lord, praise him! All you offspring
    of Jacob, glorify him;
stand in awe of him, all you offspring of Israel!
For he did not despise or abhor the affliction

of the afflicted; he did not hide his face from me,
but heard when I cried to him.

(Psalm 22.1-8, 22-24 NRSV)

I began this book with reflections on the passion of Jesus, and
I want to end there, drawing together at the same time the
various threads of the other theme that I have been trying to set
alongside it — the theme of the Church's call to serve and heal
the world, to put into effect the victory which was won on the
cross. This, in fact, is the only answer I know to the question
with which the second half of this book began: how can the
Church possibly claim that on the cross Jesus won the decisive
victory over the powers of evil?

We need to return once more to first-century Judaea, where it
all happened. Judaea had been a political football then, just as other
countries in the Middle East have become in our own day; and the
occupying forces had been there so long, and had put down all
resistance so systematically and brutally, that the ordinary people
had become either hardened into accepting the new status quo or
desperate enough to try anything. We often talk about Jesus' death
as though it happened without relation to any particular time or
place. But we can only really grasp what was going on if we think
ourselves into a situation like that of Kuwait at the start of 1991.
Imagine that; then imagine that situation continuing for a hundred
or more years; and then imagine, within that, a young charismatic
Kuwaiti leader, going round the villages away from where the troops
were stationed, getting a groundswell of local support, and finally
arriving in Kuwait city on the day that the people were, however
riskily, celebrating an ancient festival of national liberation. What
would happen? The puppet government would be deeply worried:
If this leaks out, our de facto masters will come and crush us to bits.
So they manage to arrest him away from the crowd, and hand him
over to the occupying forces as a would-be rebel leader. And the
rest is predictable.

120

This scenario makes a lot of sense. But it raises in our modern Western minds the huge question: how can something that happened two thousand years ago, in another country and another culture, be of lasting significance and value for us today? Supposing what I have just described did in fact take place, in Kuwait, or in Lebanon, or Afghanistan, or another occupied country today. Would we immediately say that therefore this moment was to be regarded as the centre of history, that everything now was different, that we in a different part of the globe would have to adjust our world-view accordingly? I think not. For that matter, when Jesus died on his cross outside Jerusalem in about AD 30, he was just one of hundreds of young Jewish rebels who died similar deaths in similar places that century. Towards the end of the great Jewish war a generation after Jesus' death, the historian Josephus, who was there and saw it all, says that there were so many crucifixions that there wasn't enough room for them all around the walls of the city. So why do we call the day of Jesus' death *Good* Friday? And why, when we speak of his death, do we talk about 'the' cross as if his were somehow different from all the others?

There are three answers which I want to offer. They are quite traditional and, in a sense, straightforward. Perhaps there is a place, at the end of a book in which I have tried to explore some less usual lines of thought, for restating some of the basics.

First, the cross of Jesus stands out because of the astonishing claims that Jesus made about the significance of what he was about to do. We know of about fifteen other messianic movements in Judaea in the two centuries surrounding Jesus' day, from about 50 BC to about AD 150. They were all without exception nationalist movements, based on a groundswell of popular expectation and zeal. None of the would-be Messiahs, so far as we have any indication at all, had any thought that their cause would come to fruition through their own death. There had been some Jews, earlier on, who when being executed by occupying forces spoke of their deaths as bringing about an end to the sufferings of Israel; but we have no mention of that in Jesus' day. Nor did such martyrs have any idea that their deaths would somehow carry significance for the wider world beyond Israel. But in Jesus' case we find, in passage after passage, that he believed himself called not only to die but to die Israel's death so that Israel would not need to die it — and to die the world's death so that the world would not need to die it.

At the heart of this extraordinary self-understanding we find his use of the Psalms. They were the prayerbook and hymnbook of ancient Israel, and wise and godly Jews of many generations had meditated on them. They included a good many passages, like the one with which I began this chapter and which Jesus quoted as he hung on the cross, which are bitter laments, poems of the suffering people of God. And we have reason to believe that Jesus, in meditating on these, had made them his own, in the sense that as he wrestled with his own strange and dark vocation he came to believe that it was somehow bound up with the destiny of the whole people of God, and that that destiny was to draw the suffering and pain and sin and death of all the world on to itself, that God's world might be healed. His fulfilment of the Scriptures was not a matter of an arbitrary acting out of a few randomly chosen prophecies, but a total obedience to the total divine plan of which these prophecies were simply symptoms.

What is the result? If we take this line we have a view of the cross which draws together so many of the popular doctrines and theories of atonement, and yet in my view transcends them. So many popular presentations are far too *abstract:* they take the whole event out of its context in history, in the story of God and his people, and imagine it simply as a nonhistorical transaction between God and Jesus into which we can somehow be slotted. But the New Testament always insists on seeing the cross as what it was — a horrible and bitter event within history; and it insists that we understand its significance within, not outside, that context. As a result, I think we are forced to say that what Jesus went to Jerusalem to do was to draw together not only, as we sing at Christmas, the hopes and fears of all the years, but also the pains and tears of all the years; they are met not simply in the little town of Bethlehem, but on the little hill of Calvary. This was Jesus' intention; and if we want to enter into it and appreciate it for ourselves we have to go in heart and mind outside the city wall, and stand or kneel before the cross, and bring the different parts of our story in front of the story which brings together God, two pieces of wood, and four strong nails. And this takes time; you can't do it in two seconds and then go away satisfied. We need to make time — carve out time, as you would for something you'd been wanting to do for months — to read slowly through the story once again and ask God to weave the story of his death into the story of our own life. And perhaps the two most helpful ways to do this are, first, to read it privately, from one or other of the Gospels, and then, second, to go to the Eucharist and realise that what you are doing is acting the story out symbolically, so that Jesus' death and your life really do become part of the same new historical reality.

But if the first answer to the question of why Jesus' cross is so important has to do with Jesus' own self-understanding as he went to his death, someone is sure to say: 'But that's all very well! Supposing Jesus was mistaken? Supposing he was after all just a deluded fanatic, with a set of bizarre fantasies about how God was to save the world?' Well, that's an option which one might reasonably take. I expect the disciples went through a stage of thinking about that in the two days following the crucifixion, and certainly a lot of hard-thinking people have done so at various stages ever since. There is no way, granted the story so far, to prove that, when Jesus died, his death had the cosmic effect he claimed it would. But of course the story doesn't end there. And so my second point is that the claim of Jesus, which he spoke of obliquely and acted out in the Last Supper, was dramatically vindicated three days later. There are many arguments for the historicity of the resurrection, and I'm not going to go into them here, except for one. People have often said that of course the disciples made up the story of Jesus' rising again; after all, their movement had failed, their hero had been executed, and cognitive dissonance set in. They couldn't cope with dashed hopes, so they invented a way of saying that he was still alive, that his defeat had after all been a victory, rather like the defeated nation that goes on proclaiming a great victory in its own media even while its troops are being defeated and decimated.

The problem with that position is as follows. We know, as I said, of about a dozen or more messianic or would-be messianic movements around the time of Jesus, and we have no indication that any of them said anything at all about their leader being still around after his death. Hezekiah, the great revolutionary in the 40s BC, was killed by Herod the Great: his followers didn't claim he'd been raised from the dead. Judas, his son, led a messianic movement after the death of Herod; after his death, nobody claimed to have seen him alive. An ex-slave called Simon was proclaimed king in around 4 BC, and when the Romans killed him no movement arose to commemorate him. A shepherd called Athronges was crowned by a group of followers at the same time, and he went the same way. In the decade or two after Jesus' death there were three or four other messianic leaders; they were either cut down by troops or crucified, and nobody said they had risen from the dead three days later. During the war a generation after Jesus' time there were two more great revolutionary king-figures, another Simon and a descendent of Hezekiah and Judas called Menahem; Simon was captured by the Romans and executed, and Menahem was killed by a rival group of Jews. Nobody claimed to have seen them alive, and eaten in their company, a few days later. Two generations after that Simeon ben-Kosiba was hailed as Israel's Messiah. He led a glorious three-year guerrilla resistance movement, before finally being caught and killed by the Romans. No sect arose claiming to have been witnesses that God had raised him from the dead.

But within a short while of the crucifixion of Jesus of Nazareth, his disciples, who had been defeated and bedraggled just before, appeared in public in front of their countrymen claiming that they had seen Jesus, that they had spoken with him, that God had brought him through death and out the other side into a new dimension of life over which death no longer had any authority. And they saw this without a shadow of doubt as the vindication of his claim — that his death really had been the turning point of history, the moment around which all other moments must now regroup themselves. It is the resurrection that gives the answer to the sceptic's question about Jesus' view of his own death. And it is therefore the resurrection, and the meaning which it gives to the cross, which is the ground of Christian *assurance*. People often ask, 'How can I *know* that God loves *me*, that I too am saved, that I am a member of his redeemed family?' The answer is that as long as you are looking inside yourself, you will have doubts. But as long as you are looking at Jesus on his cross, and seeing that event in the light of his resurrection, you can be assured that this was done for you too; that the story of God which encompasses wood, nails, and an empty tomb can become, and indeed must become, the basis and groundplan for the story of your life as well.

But if this is so there remains a third point, which we can get at by means of another question. Does all of this mean that the cross is after all an abstract event, which, although it sits there in the middle of history, only affects individuals when they look at it in faith? To put the question another way round, and to return to the question of several chapters ago: if Jesus came to live and die and rise again in order to save the world from sin and evil, doesn't this mean that he was after all a failure? Isn't there just as much sin and evil in the world today as there was then?

Well, I don't know the answer to that last question. I don't know how you might go about quantifying sin and evil, and that's perhaps not a helpful thing to try to do in any case. But I do know this. When Jesus explained his own mission and goal, he continually told parables which spoke of a gradual process; a mustard seed which starts small and gets bigger, a secret treasure which people go and buy, a seed growing secretly until the time of harvest. He does not seem to have intended a sudden total reversal, which would in any case entail blotting out human responsibility and starting again from scratch. He chose a different route; that in his dying and rising he would call men and women to share a new life, a new way of being human, a new way of healing the world — and would commission them to go out with an agenda similar to his, to *implement* the work of the cross in all the world.

And this is where the story of the cross becomes, if we will let it, the story of our life as well. When Jesus calls us to bear the cross throughout our lives, he is not calling us merely to private asceticism, as though our only purpose were to cultivate our own holiness and salvation. Indeed, if you focus on your own salvation to the exclusion of all else you are almost certainly looking in the wrong direction. Rather, he calls us to share in his work of drawing out and dealing with the evil of the world; by loving our neighbours, both immediate and far off, with the strong love that sent him to the cross; and by working out the implications of that love in our own vocations, whatever they may be, in our social and political action, in our relationships (and particularly our marriages and families), and in our caring for those in our midst who need the healing and restoring love of God most deeply. We are called, as the people who claim the crucified Jesus as our Lord, to seek out the pain of the world, and, in prayer, in patient hard work, in listening, in healing, in announcing the Kingdom of this Jesus by every means possible, to take that pain into ourselves and give it over to Jesus himself so that the world may be healed.

We are called, therefore, to claim the cross as the victory which undergirds all our work for God. Without it, we would find the odds against us far too heavy, and would be totally discouraged; or we might imagine that our own goodness, or political skill, or human shrewdness, or sheer power would eradicate evil from the world. With the cross as the underlying story of our lives, validated by the resurrection and then implemented by the fire of the Holy Spirit, we can have the confidence to take on the world with the sovereign love of God. 'In the world,' said Jesus, 'you have tribulation. But be of good cheer: I have overcome the world.'

Almighty God, you gave up your only begotten Son Jesus Christ to a shameful death, that we sinners might find in him our life and our peace: grant to us, we pray, such an understanding of that death, and of the love which it embodied, that we may give to him and, through him, to you, the worship and love of our hearts and our lives, that by the power of your Spirit your healing love may flow, through us, to your world: through the same your son Jesus Christ our Lord, to whom with you and the Holy Spirit be all glory, now and for ever. Amen.